GW00724541

PENGUIN BOOKS

LADY TRAVELLERS

Bee Dawson is a New Zealand writer with a special interest in gardens, plants and social history. She regularly contributes to *New Zealand Gardener* and other magazines and has previously published *Lady Painters, the Flower Painters of Early New Zealand* for Penguin. She lives in Wellington with her husband and two school-age children.

LADY TRAVELLERS
THE TOURISTS OF EARLY NEW ZEALAND

BEE DAWSON

PENGUIN BOOKS

CONTENTS

ACKNOWLEDGEMENTS

A BOOK SUCH AS THIS IS NEVER POSSIBLE WITHOUT SIGNIFICANT INPUT FROM MANY PEOPLE OTHER THAN THE AUTHOR. I WOULD ESPECIALLY LIKE TO THANK MY PUBLISHER, BERNICE BEACHMAN, WHO had the initial foresight and enthusiasm to commission *Lady Travellers*.

Research is a crucial part of any such exercise, the people who keep the collections an essential support in producing stories of any past lives. I am indebted to Marian Minson, Curator of Drawings and Prints at the Alexander Turnbull Library, for once again giving me generous support and advice, as well as helping me source many of the illustrations in this book.

I have greatly appreciated the help afforded me by many other staff in the Alexander Turnbull Library, especially David Colquhoun and his team in the Manuscripts and Archives Section, and Joan McCracken, Research Librarian of the Turnbull Library Pictures. Similarly, the National Library staff were ever helpful. I gratefully acknowledge Glenda Gale's wizardry at defining dates.

At the Museum of New Zealand Te Papa Tongarewa, Tony Mackle, Collection Manager of Prints and Drawings, Bronwyn Labrum, Curator of History and Textiles, and Valerie Carson, Conservator of Textiles, generously shared their time and treasures with me. What they produced gave inspiration as much as illustration.

Thank you also to Kerry McCarthy, Curator of Pictures at Canterbury Museum, for helping me to find wonderful photographs of mountaineering women; to Neil Roberts, Curator of the Robert McDougall Art Gallery in Christchurch, for his assistance with my research on Caroline Chevalier; to Anne McEwen of the Nelson Provincial Museum for her help with Constance Barnicoat, and to the staff at the Auckland Public Library for showing me papers relevant to Sarah Mathew.

Charlotte MacDonald, Head of the History Department at Victoria University, kindly gave me her support and advice. This was also generously provided, along with specialist proofreading, by mountaineering historian Graham Langton.

Isabel Scott deserves a special mention for introducing me to the story of Betsey Broughton, the famed forebear of her children's nanny. In addition, Isabel provided me with relevant family histories, essential references for this extraordinary tale.

Thank you to Joanna Woods for introducing me to the story of the Dobie sisters. Their illustrated shipboard diary and the tale of poor Mary's brutal end were so fascinating that the book was suddenly expanded to accommodate this material. I also appreciate the generosity of Margaret Drake Brockman and Katherine Proby, great-great-nieces of Mary and Bertha Dobie, in allowing me to use the written and pictorial material from the diary.

The most delightful travel account is undoubtedly that of the three Richardson sisters, Victorian tomboys adventuring in the sub-antarctic. Cynthia Cass, granddaughter of the oldest sister, most generously lent me her great aunt's 'ship's log' and helped me ensure that my account was as accurate as possible.

I would like to thank Philippa Gerrard for project-managing the book's progress from computer to published work. Her patience and good humour are ever impressive. Thank you also to Pat Field who edited the text with care and sensitivity, and to Athena Sommerfeld for the elegant design.

Once again friends have provided humour, warmth and wine. Thank you to Wendy McGuinness for her initial inspiration for *Lady Travellers*, to Murray and Erin at Millwood Books for ongoing thoughts, and to Penny Deans for yet more logistic and proofreading support. My sister, Stella Clark, has once more been a paragon of proofreading precision.

And a special thank you to my husband, Sandy, and children, James and Laura, for their patience, good humour and ability to adapt their lives to literary demands. The meals may not always have been on time, but the manuscript was!

INTRODUCTION

NINETEENTH-CENTURY NEW ZEALAND: LAND OF MAORI, MOUNTAINS, FIORDS, FORESTS AND GEYSERS, AN EXOTIC, FAR-FLUNG FRONTIER OF THE BRITISH EMPIRE. RAW IN ITS COLONIAL DEVELOPMENT, AND kinder than many other lands, it proved irresistibly attractive to explorers, missionaries, naturalists and settlers: travellers of every persuasion. To get there, European men and women braved ships and seas as few of us would contemplate today, venturing intrepidly to this strange southern land. Once in New Zealand, the travelling continued as European visitors converted the 'heathen', surveyed the terrain, took up land, fought bloody battles and strove to establish a familiar 'civilisation'. In later years, voyages to the Antipodes developed a more frivolous appeal: New Zealand was undeniably an alluring destination for those with the money and freedom to travel.

The difficulty has not been in finding women to include in this book, but rather in narrowing down the potential list of 'lady travellers' to a selected few. During my research I found many fascinating lives, scores of tales that could have merited inclusion. In the end I have largely restricted my selection to a small number of those who travelled from choice rather than necessity. My 'lady travellers' were the early explorers and tourists of colonial New Zealand.

The one exception is Betsey Broughton who came to New Zealand briefly as a two-year-old, survived a massacre and saw her mother killed and eaten by local Maori. Once rescued, it took a further two and a half extraordinary years before she was returned home to Australia. Betsey's experiences were so remarkable, the story so fascinating, that I felt compelled to include her in this book.

Surveyor's wife Sarah Mathew exemplifies the adventurous spirit of many pioneering lady travellers. Rather than staying in the comparative safety of the Bay of Islands, she determined to travel with her husband as much as possible. Sarah sailed around New Zealand in unsavoury ships, camped on unknown shores, and was generally undaunted by the prospect of meeting reputedly ferocious Maori. Sarah never complained and avidly recorded all her experiences in her journal.

Life for a travelling 'lady' was undoubtedly better than for a woman of working class. Her character may have been no finer, but her berth invariably was. There was more money for 'luxury' cabin accommodation and good food, the wherewithal for the better hotels. This did not, however, mean that a lady always travelled in style. Caroline Chevalier, the wife of a prominent Melbourne artist, cheerfully adapted to the challenge of travelling through rough mountain and bush terrain for weeks on end, her personal effects little more than a riding habit and one silk dress. It is remarkable that a young woman used to only the most genteel forms of exercise was fit enough for such a major expedition.

Immigrants apart, 'lady travellers' seldom had children. Practical realities certainly militated against such freedom of movement for mothers: travelling for enjoyment, with or without husbands, was generally an option only for the childless. The notable exception in the book is Constance, Lady Ranfurly, who had the rare privilege of travelling with extensive viceregal trappings, happily supported by aides-de-camp, governesses, butlers, cooks and footmen as she accompanied her husband on his gubernatorial duties.

The reasons for the childlessness of the other women are varied: although no hint is given as to why the Chevaliers did not have children, we know that Sarah Mathew was plagued with miscarriages, while age may have been an issue for the late-marrying Constance Barnicoat. As women who preferred to form close relationships with members of their own sex, Constance Astley and Freda du Faur were never likely to marry and produce families.

I was especially fascinated by our early 'lady mountaineers', women who ventured into the New Zealand alps wearing the most impractical of clothes. These remarkable characters often had to fight against conventional social mores before they could brave the elements and take up the challenges of alpine adventure. There were many of these women and it was frustrating not to be able to tell more of their stories.

I am especially indebted to those who recorded at least parts of their tales in writing or art – their efforts left rich stories for later telling. Where possible, paintings and drawings by the women have been included, along with much of their writing. This gives a keen sense of 'here and now', a feeling of close connection that brings their adventures to life a century or more later.

It has been a fascinating task to research and write of such adventurous lives. In an age where travel is relatively cheap and easy it is sometimes hard to imagine exactly how brave our early travelling ladies were. These were resilient, gutsy women who, revelling in their escape from the polite parlours of society, hitched up their skirts and determinedly grasped a slice of adventure. I salute them.

Bee Dawson
Wellington, April 2001

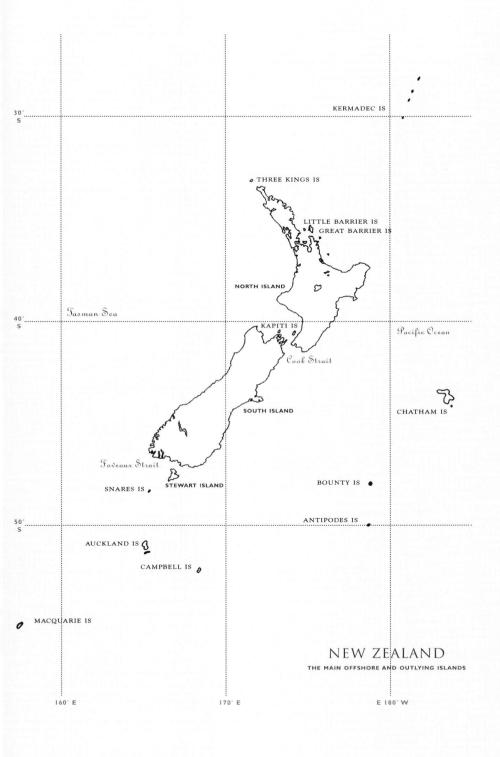

KERMADEC IS

THREE KINGS IS

LITTLE BARRIER IS
GREAT BARRIER IS

NORTH ISLAND

Tasman Sea

KAPITI IS

Pacific Ocean

Cook Strait

CHATHAM IS

SOUTH ISLAND

Foveaux Strait

SNARES IS   STEWART ISLAND   BOUNTY IS

ANTIPODES IS

AUCKLAND IS

CAMPBELL IS

MACQUARIE IS

NEW ZEALAND
THE MAIN OFFSHORE AND OUTLYING ISLANDS

160° E   170° E   E 180° W

30°
S

40°
S

50°
S

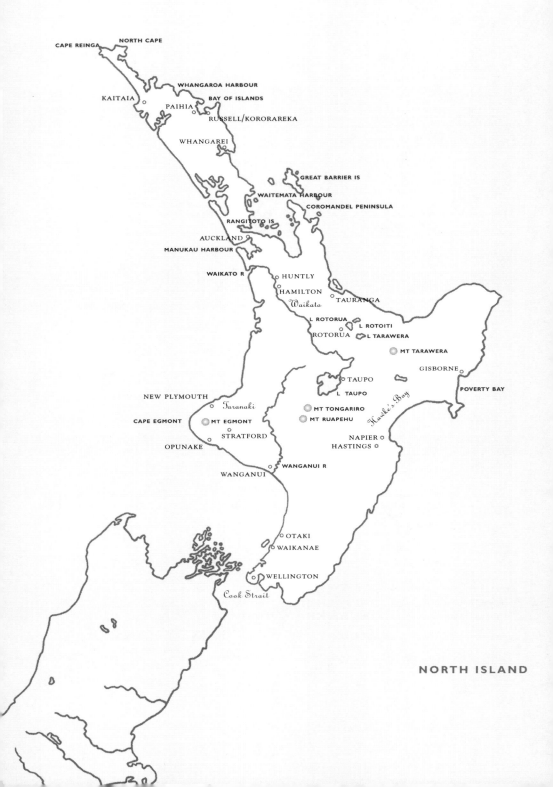

CAPE REINGA • NORTH CAPE

WHANGAROA HARBOUR
KAITAIA • BAY OF ISLANDS
PAIHIA •
RUSSELL/KORORAREKA

WHANGAREI

GREAT BARRIER IS
WAITEMATA HARBOUR
COROMANDEL PENINSULA
RANGITOTO IS
AUCKLAND •
MANUKAU HARBOUR

WAIKATO R
HUNTLY •
HAMILTON •
Waikato
TAURANGA

L ROTORUA
L ROTOITI
ROTORUA • L TARAWERA

MT TARAWERA •
GISBORNE
TAUPO •
L TAUPO
POVERTY BAY

NEW PLYMOUTH
Taranaki
MT TONGARIRO •
MT RUAPEHU •
CAPE EGMONT
MT EGMONT •
STRATFORD
NAPIER
OPUNAKE
HASTINGS

WANGANUI R
WANGANUI

OTAKI
WAIKANAE

WELLINGTON
Cook Strait

Hawke's Bay

NORTH ISLAND

NEW ZEALAND

0   100   200   300

KM

MARLBOROUGH SOUNDS

GOLDEN BAY

TOTARANUI

NELSON   PICTON

Marlborough

BLENHEIM

Cook Strait

WESTPORT

West Coast

GREYMOUTH

TARAMAKAU R

HOKITIKA

L BRUNNER

KANIERE R

OTIRA GORGE

ARTHUR'S PASS

L KANIERE

HURUNUI R

L COLERIDGE

WAIMAKARIRI R

Southern Alps

CHRISTCHURCH

PIGEON BAY

LYTTELTON

GOVERNORS BAY

OKAINS BAY

AKAROA

L TEKAPO

THE HERMITAGE

COPLAND PASS

TASMAN GLACIER

HOOKER R

MT COOK

JACKSON BAY

FAIRLIE

Canterbury Plains

TIMARU

L WANAKA

L HAWEA

MILFORD SOUND

GEORGE SOUND

L WAKATIPU

QUEENSTOWN

RANFURLY

CROMWELL

L TE ANAU

ALEXANDRA

Otago

L MANAPOURI

DUNEDIN

Fiordland

Southland

INVERCARGILL

CLUTHA R

BLUFF

STEWART IS

PORT PEGASUS

SOUTH ISLAND

BETSEY BROUGHTON
1807 – 1891
THE BURNING OF THE BOYD

AS SHE ATTEMPTED TO FOLLOW THE WOMAN AND CHILD, A MAORI LUNGED AT ELIZABETH WITH HIS KNIFE, SLASHING AT THE BABY IN HER ARMS. THE RAZOR SHARP BLADE SLICED THROUGH THE TINY BODY AND penetrated his mother's left breast. She reeled back, the lifeless body of her baby slipping to her feet. Her scream choked into silence as the savage fell on her again hacking her to death, flaying her body and limbs. Her blood sprayed over Betsy's long white frock as the little girl wrenched herself free from Mrs Morley and rushed back towards her mother …

… From the decks came dreadful screams from passengers and crew … Many cries were mingled with terrified pleas for pity, but their killers kept up awful war-cries as they systematically went about their grisly slaughter. Mrs Morley could not blot from her mind what she had witnessed before escaping with Betsy … She had seen the murdering cannibal lift the quivering flesh of her friend to his blood-stained mouth while Elizabeth's dying scream was still ringing in her ears.[1]

[1] Lorna Howlett, *The Throsbys of Throsby Park*. Published in Australia by Del Throsby, 1991, p. 37.

This imaginative reconstruction of the death of Elizabeth Broughton during the sacking of the trading brig, the *Boyd*, in Whangaroa Harbour in late 1809 is perhaps over-dramatised, but most of the lurid details of the scene are probably correct. Mrs Morley survived the massacre, and this particular story is likely to owe much to her later account of the tragedy.

There is some embellishment though. Although there is no doubt that the crew and passengers were eaten by their attackers, raw flesh was never on the menu. A later report by the rescuer of the survivors, Alexander Berry, notes that these Maori 'had massacred, roasted and eaten forty of my countrymen'. The bodies were dismembered and cooked before they were consumed.

Elizabeth was the common-law wife of William Broughton, one-time servant to the ship's surgeon aboard the convict transport *Charlotte* and later the deputy commissary at Sydney. Known either as Elizabeth Heathorn or Ann Glossop, she was a former convict who had met her husband some sixteen years previously, shortly after transportation to Sydney.

Known facts are few, but family tradition suggests that Elizabeth was arrested when some stolen cloth was found in her bag. Although claiming her innocence of the crime, she was unable to contact her employers and had no money to bribe her way to freedom as other young women may have been able to do. Elizabeth had no option but to stand trial.

The lack of young single women in New South Wales was of concern to the British government at that time. Elizabeth's fate was sealed when an order came through that any young women who were under arrest, and were strong enough to stand the trip, were to be sentenced to immediate transportation. The young Elizabeth was sentenced at Welshpool, Montgomeryshire, to transportation for seven years. She arrived in Sydney in the *Pitt* in February 1792.

With a lack of 'respectable' women in the colony, liaisons between convicts and government employees were not uncommon – the attachment that soon formed between the convict, Elizabeth Heathorn, and the Parramatta storekeeper, William Broughton, would have raised few eyebrows. However, the unforgiving attitude of the colony's clergy dissuaded the couple from any formal marriage that might have brought disrepute to William. It is particularly telling that, while in Sydney, the Broughtons were refused a Christian baptism for their first two children.

Although the marriage was never formalised in the eyes of the church or

A view of the southern part of Sydney. *After C.A. Lesueur, 1802.*
Sydney as it would have appeared to the Broughtons in their early years in the settlement.

the law, it appears to have been a happy union. Obviously devoted to both Elizabeth and his children, William lived openly with his family. When William was appointed commissary of the convict settlement at Norfolk Island the family moved with him. Here, attitudes were a little more relaxed and the resident chaplain happily christened the two older children as well as the next two born during the Broughtons' stay on the island. The fifth and youngest child, Elizabeth Isabella or Betsey, born on Norfolk Island on 14 November 1807, was christened back in Sydney. By the time it was Betsey's turn to face the font the colonial church had become a little more pragmatic.

When the Norfolk Island establishment was reduced, Broughton was discharged. He then took his family to Sydney where he was appointed deputy commissary of stores in New South Wales at a wage of five shillings a day. Over the next few years he spent significant periods as acting commissary and was warmly praised by Governor Macquarie for his diligence and honesty. He was made a magistrate in 1809.

The ship in which the Broughton family returned to Sydney was the *City of Edinburgh*, owned by ship's surgeon turned entrepreneur, Alexander Berry, who had accepted a commission to evacuate settlers from Norfolk Island to Van Diemen's Land. Berry and the Broughtons became friendly during the voyage and, once back in Sydney, Berry was a frequent visitor at the

Broughton home. The Broughtons also readily made friends with 'establishment' families, who appeared to be entirely unconcerned about either Elizabeth's convict origins or the lack of a formal marriage contract. In particular they became close to Charles Throsby, landowner, explorer, surgeon and magistrate, and his wife Jane.

William not only regarded his children with the greatest of affection, he also did his utmost to ensure that they were given the best upbringing and education possible. It was a tough time for devoted parents, but the Broughtons were only too well aware that their children's future prospects were very limited if they stayed in Australia. An English education was essential if the young Broughtons were to advance well in the world and by 1808 William and Elizabeth's older children were back in England. This was a major undertaking as just the journey 'Home' could take as long as six months and future communication was sure to be most infrequent. The children are likely to have lived with relations of William in Kent, attending schools nearby.

Then, in 1809, Elizabeth had a sixth child: a baby boy. It seemed an opportune time for her to take a trip back to England to visit Mary Ann, now sixteen, ten-year-old Sarah and the seven-year-old William. Rebecca, who was five, was still in Sydney and was to be cared for in Elizabeth's absence by a widowed friend, but two-year-old Betsey was to travel with her mother and baby brother.

Elizabeth and these two youngest children were among the passengers who boarded the Boyd on November 8, 1809. Commanded by Captain John Thompson, the 600-ton Boyd was an impressive ship, boasting twin masts, three decks and a generous 30-foot beam. She was loaded with a cargo of Australian coal, hardwood, whale oil and seal skins, and carried a number of passengers. The ship's complement included four Maori men who were working their passage home to New Zealand.

When the Boyd left Sydney it had just one further port of call before making its way around Cape Horn to Cape Town and finally England. The visit to Whangaroa Harbour in northern New Zealand was well planned, calculated to complete the cargo with a load of kauri spars. Whangaroa was a relatively novel port of call – the Boyd would be only the third European ship to load kauri here.

We know little about the journey to New Zealand. However, accounts tell that at least one of the four Maori sailors on board was mistreated during the voyage. Most notably, a young chief, 'George' or Te Aara, was flogged, probably on three separate occasions, for misdemeanours he did not commit. One was when the cook accidentally threw a dozen pewter spoons belonging to the captain overboard: George was quickly blamed and the captain ordered that he be punished by the boatswain. When George protested that he was a chief and therefore should not be flogged, Captain Thompson replied that he was a 'cokey' (slave). Captain Thompson was also reported as having flogged George from his sickbed in order to force him back to work. Hard for any sailor to suffer, but much worse for George whose chiefly mana was once again terribly affronted.

It was hardly surprising that when the *Boyd* arrived at Whangaroa, George and his fellow sailors told their friends and relatives of their experiences, George bitterly displaying his lacerated back. Revenge was probably inevitable – it was decided to take the ship as 'utu'.

The following account, published in the *Sydney Gazette* on 4 September 1810, almost a year after the massacre, is probably the most accurate tale of the events.

Captain Thompson was invited ashore and went, taking three armed boats. Once in the bush he and his men were confronted by their Maori shipmates who upbraided them for their mistreatment. When Thompson turned to go back to the ship, he and his men were attacked with clubs and axes, and killed and later eaten. The warriors returned to the ship in darkness, dressed in their victims' clothes, and told the second officer that Thompson had decided to sleep on shore but told them to begin loading the spars on board. They came over the side and attacked the rest of the crew, who were soon all killed, except for a few who ran up the rigging and stayed there all night. One man was sent to call the passengers up on deck to look at the spars being loaded, and they were also killed. Only a woman and her two children, who had hidden below, and the boy Davis were saved.

The next morning, when Te Pahi arrived at the ship, he was angry about what had happened. He tried to save the men in the rigging, telling them

George

Second in Rank, and Brother to the New Zealand King Tabooha, at the Wesleyan missionary Settlement, Wesley Dale, Warngeroa New Zealand

Samuel Leigh. 1823

George, Second in Rank and Brother to the New Zealand King Tabooha.
Attributed to Samuel Leigh, 1823.

PRIVATE COLLECTION. ON LOAN TO THE AUCKLAND ART GALLERY TOI O TAMAKI.

that if they could get to his canoe, he would rescue them. They made the attempt but were intercepted and killed while Te Pahi was held back forcibly.

The woman and two children were then taken ashore and the ship plundered. Te Pahi was allowed to take away three boatloads of goods from the ship, except the guns, which the local people kept for themselves. One man, who was anxious to test a musket he had taken, snapped it over a cask of powder, which blew up, killing five local women and eight or nine men and setting fire to the Boyd.

It is important to view the massacre of the *Boyd's* crew and passengers and the plundering of the ship in the context of the times. Europeans were still an alien presence in New Zealand, the early years of the nineteenth century being marked only spasmodically by visits of whalers and trading ships. From early 1808 onwards relationships were deteriorating, with ill will and violent incidents typical of all parties.

It is fair to say that the itinerant sailors, sealers and whalers were a particularly lawless group of men who readily exploited and antagonised the Maori people. In 1808 the missionary James Elder noted how potato plantations and storehouses were regularly raided by sailors while local natives who were enticed on board ships and lured below decks were stripped of their possessions.

When they complained [the whalers] Beat them severly [sic] and sent them ashore Strip'd and weeping; and at that time the Natives of the Bay of Islands, were very friendly, and very ready to supply every refreshments to the Ships in their power. I was often surprised from the ill treatment I saw them receive, they did not raise and murder us all. I have no doubt that the Natives would be kind and attentive to the Crews of the Ships that put in there, if they were treated with any degree of common Justice honesty and civility.

It is hardly surprising that the 'Natives' were not always so tolerant. In early 1808 local people gladly supplied food to the crew of the *Parramatta*, but

25

instead of receiving payment they were thrown overboard and shot at. Several were wounded. Small wonder that, when the *Parramatta* later ran aground, the crew were all killed and the ship plundered.

Humiliation of local chiefs was also all too common. In February or March of 1808 the prominent local Bay of Islands chief Te Pahi or Tippahee (later mentioned in the 1810 *Sydney Gazette* report of the attack on the *Boyd*) was accused of stealing one of twenty baskets of potatoes traded for nails on the *Elizabeth*. The enraged Captain lashed Te Pahi to the ship's rigging for five or six hours, an appalling affront to the mana of any chief. When it was discovered that the basket had, in fact, been stolen by one of the ship's sailors, no apology was forthcoming.

This self-same Te Pahi had previously enjoyed excellent relationships with the Europeans, being a friend of both the missionary Samuel Marsden and Philip King, the governor of New South Wales, and was well used to meeting 'rangatira to rangatira'. In 1805 he and a group of his tribesmen stayed for several months in Sydney, exchanging gifts with Governor King whom he greatly impressed. Te Pahi was later described by one cabin boy, Jacky Marmon: '– His countenance was expressive of much intelligence, his manners were affable, and in every way he seemed anxious to evince his regard and esteem for the pakeha … He was one of the finest natives it ever was my fortune to meet.'

The tale of the burning of the *Boyd* must now pass to Alexander Berry, friend of the Broughton family and owner of the *City of Edinburgh*, also trading in northern New Zealand waters. The *City of Edinburgh* had come in search of kauri spars, in firm demand with the English navy at the Cape of Good Hope.

Berry's first intimation that anything was wrong was when the *City of Edinburgh* was lying at anchorage at Kororareka in the Bay of Islands. One of the friendly local chiefs, Tara, brought him the news that the people of Whangaroa had captured a ship, that they had killed and eaten all the crew and taken all the muskets and gunpowder. What is more, it was said that they were planning to come south to Kororareka to attack the *City of Edinburgh*. Although the report was initially disbelieved, rumours were sufficiently persistent for Berry to take a party to investigate.

Once the boats were anchored inside the Whangaroa Heads, Berry's party soon encountered two Ngaati Uru chiefs, newly clad in clothes made from the

Portrait of Alexander Berry.
P3/B, MITCHELL LIBRARY, STATE LIBRARY OF NEW
SOUTH WALES.

Boyd's canvas. These chiefs, Te Puhi and Te Aara (the 'George' who had been so badly treated), are likely to have been the two main instigators of the incident. There was no question of denial – they freely admitted to the attack on the *Boyd*, proudly boasting of their exploits.

Once Berry heard that there were survivors of the massacre he offered these chiefs an ultimatum – they could accept some axes he had brought in exchange for the safe delivery of the survivors, or else the chiefs would be attacked and killed. The pragmatic Te Puhi didn't take a lot of persuading. He quickly remarked that 'trading was better than fighting', and invited Berry and his crew to visit his settlement.

Insisting that the chiefs remain in his boat as hostages, Berry and his men rowed up a narrow, winding river past mangrove-lined shores hiding musket-firing warriors. Given the reported brutality of recent events, the small ship's party must have felt extraordinarily vulnerable.

Once in the bay, a fearful sight greeted Berry and his compatriots. He later reported that the wreck of the *Boyd*, burnt to the waterline, lay in the shallow water with 'the mangled fragments and fresh bones of our countrymen,

Enlèvement du *Boyd* par les Nouveaux Zélandais. *Louis Auguste de Sainson, 1839.*
PUBL-0034-2-390, ALEXANDER TURNBULL LIBRARY, WELLINGTON.

with the marks even of the teeth remaining upon them'.

Among the waiting crowd, European clothing was well in evidence, proudly worn by the women of the village. It is hardly surprising that the invitation of overnight accommodation was firmly refused. The Europeans gladly forfeited the promise of comfort for a night on a small, rugged island.

In the morning Berry's party was brought the one surviving woman passenger, Mrs Morley (a publican's wife from Sydney) along with her baby and a boy, Thomas Davis. They were told that young Thomas had survived because he had managed to hide in the hold for several days, whereas Mrs Morley had had pity taken on her by an old 'savage' moved by her tears and embraces. Elsewhere it is reported that Mrs Morley and the children escaped death because of intervention by Maori women: 'These the women of the Nga-ti-uru saved in spite of the men of the tribe.'

Some later reports suggest that Davis was spared because he was kind to George, while another source suggests that it was because Davis had a club-foot and the Maori took him to be 'a son of the devil'.

The chiefs were given their axes, but then Mrs Morley told Berry of two more survivors; one, the second mate, the other, little Betsey Broughton. When pressed, the principal chief told Berry that the second mate had initially been kept alive to make fish hooks out of iron hoops. A disappointing venture for all as he proved no good at the task, so he was duly killed and eaten. However, Betsey was still thought to be alive and in the possession of a chief whose pa was on an island at the entrance to the harbour.

Stating that the girl was his 'brother's daughter' Berry held a gun to the chief's head. The two chiefs and their attendants were forced into the boat and were rowed to the island where the chiefs were held hostage while one of their attendants was sent ashore. After another interval Berry ordered the principal chief to send a further message. If the child was not immediately brought to him, both chiefs would be shot and everyone on the island would be killed.

At this, the chief 'gave me a most ferocious look, his eyes became blood-shot and resembled the eyes of a Tiger springing on its prey'. Berry drew his sword and pointed it at the chief's chest and the chief began to cry.

This threat had the desired effect as, shortly afterwards, the second man went ashore and returned with Betsey. The little girl was clean, dressed in a linen shirt that had belonged to the *Boyd*'s captain, and wearing white feathers in her hair. However, her general physical condition was poor, she was very thin and there were sores all over her body.

Her father, William Broughton, later wrote:

In a few hours, to the agreeable astonishment of Mr Berry she was produced and, although the child was in a very emaciated state, it still afforded him much pleasure for she was the Daughter of his Friend. By the intrepidity and courage of this worthy man the Child's Life was preserved for owing to the unwholesome food of which from necessity she had been obliged to partake during her stay in common with the savages, it occasioned a disease which must have inevitably put a period to her existence had she remained with them but a few days longer.

Berry reports that Betsey called out feebly, in a complaining tone, 'Mamma, my Mamma!' Later, when asked what had happened to her mother, she drew her hands across her throat, saying she had been cut up, cooked and eaten.

Despite strong pressure from his men to kill all the natives on the island, Berry refused, regarding such an action as cowardly. Instead he took the two chiefs to the Bay of Islands, keeping them captive until he was given the ship's papers. When the *Boyd*'s papers arrived three days later, Berry was particularly gratified to find that they included some Bills of Exchange he had been sending to his agents in London.

On reflection, Berry was discontent with the punishment meted out to the chiefs. All hands were summoned and Berry announced his intentions:

> If an Englishman committed a single murder, he was hanged, [but] they had massacred a whole Ships Crew and therefore could expect no mercy but as they were Chiefs I would not degrade them by hanging but would shoot them.

Two muskets were brought, loaded by Berry and handed to two Pacific Islanders on the crew. They aimed carefully and fired, but the chiefs stood unharmed – Berry had only loaded the guns with powder. The terrified chiefs were extraordinarily relieved when their real punishment was revealed – to be slaves for the rest of their lives, destined to wait on Matengaro, a chief friendly to the Europeans.

Initially, 'that old rascal Tippahee [Te Pahi], who has been so much and so undeservedly caressed at Port Jackson' was held to blame for the *Boyd* massacre. Certainly his public humiliations may have given him some cause, though his ongoing relationships with Europeans had been generally co-operative.

However, later accounts, including a version told by Te Pahi's Ngati Pou rivals, apportion the blame elsewhere. Irrespective of who initiated the attack, the initial popular perception was that Te Pahi was behind the burning of the *Boyd* and the massacre of the crew and passengers – certainly he shared in the plunder. Retaliation was inevitable and when the crews of six whalers sacked his pa the following year, Te Pahi was wounded. Although he later recovered he was killed in battle with the Ngati Pou within the year.

In contrast to popular opinion, prominent missionary Samuel Marsden, along with a number of his colleagues, consistently supported Te Pahi, seeing him 'as innocent and noble, a victim of brutal degraded Europeans'.[2]

[2] Anne Salmond, *Between Worlds*. Viking, 1997, p. 388.

Although the *City of Edinburgh* left the Bay of Islands shortly after the rescue expedition at the end of January or beginning of February 1810, there was no quick return home for Betsey. The ship was South America bound, sailing first to Valparaiso and then to Lima. Here, Berry instructed his agent to find a family whom he could pay to look after Betsey.

This was quickly done; the agent, Mr Ferrer, reported that although 'the ladies in Lima were generally rather bad', he knew a wealthy merchant whose family would be only too happy to take care of the little girl. Payment was regarded as entirely unnecessary. Mr Ferrer assured Berry: 'Oh never mind ... Mrs Rico is a very amiable lady, and as she has no children, is delighted with the idea of having a child to care for.'

Berry continues: 'A mutual attachment grew between the child and Mrs Rico and even Mr Rico became as much attached to the little girl as his lady. Both he and Mrs Rico made me many overtures to leave the child with them for a few years but the father of the child was a friend of mine and I considered it a duty to do my best to restore her to him.'

Even so, Betsey lived with the Ricos for almost a year before she was reluctantly parted from this warm-hearted Spanish family. When her former protector, Mrs Morley, became sick and died at Lima (Alexander Berry notes: 'It is supposed as a consequence of her own irregularities with the crew') her baby was also cared for by a Spanish family.

That the Ricos treated Betsey well is clearly borne out by the letter Betsey's father wrote some years later to accompany a portrait of his daughter. In this letter he 'most respectfully inscribes this portrait to Don Gaspardo Rico and the other Spanish Gentlemen and Ladies as a tribute of respect and grateful remembrance for so nobly distinguishing themselves by their humanity in their protection and benevolent treatment of the Child during her residence at Lima for eleven months'.

When Berry eventually sailed for Rio de Janeiro he took both Betsey and little Miss Morley with him. In Rio an acquaintance of William Broughton, the captain of the British brig the *Atlanta*, 'offered to take charge of Betsey Broughton' and Berry 'agreed on condition of his taking also the other little girl ... saved along with her to her father'.

Twenty years later Berry wrote: 'It was fortunate that I did not leave these children at Lima for some time after the Revolution commenced.' This revolution did not serve the Ricos well. Don Gaspar Rico was an 'old Spaniard', very active in the Loyalist party. Along with other loyalists, Rico was blockaded in the Castle of Callao during a time of 'such privation that a rat was sold for an ounce of gold'. He and many others perished of hunger. It is not known what happened to Betsey's surrogate mother, the warm-hearted Mrs Rico, but it is probable that she met a similar fate.

As for the other survivors: Berry relates that the baby, 'Miss Morley', returned to Australia with Betsey. Here she lived with her sister and in later years kept a school in Sydney. When she gave up the school she lived on a property inherited from her publican father.

Young Thomas Davis left Lima for London on the *Archduke Charles*, returning to work with his old master shortly after his arrival in England. When Alexander Berry saw him again, some eleven years later, Davis pleaded to be able to return to Australia with Berry. He did so, but lost his life when exploring the coast north of Sydney.

The first that Betsey's father, William Broughton, would have known of the disaster that had befallen his family was some four months after the *Boyd* had sailed for London. By this point he would have been quietly confident that Elizabeth, his baby son and beloved daughter were well on their way to a fond reunion with the Broughtons' English-educated children. Then, on 9 March 1810, word of the burning of the *Boyd* and the massacre of the crew and passengers finally arrived at Port Jackson, brought by Captain Chace of the *King George*.

William's horror and subsequent despair at the awful fate of his wife and son would have been softened to a degree by the seemingly miraculous escape of Betsey. He must have longed to see his little daughter again as quickly as possible, to hold his beloved child in his arms, to reassure himself that she really had survived. If he had known that over two more years would pass before their reunion, it could only have compounded his misery.

William was now confronted with the miserable prospect of writing to his children in England to explain that their beloved mother would not be coming to see them. It must have been even harder to tell them why; that she and their baby brother were cruelly murdered, hacked to death, roasted and eaten, their bones left to lie on a savage shore. There was not even the consolation of Elizabeth and the baby having had a Christian burial.

Left: Portrait of Elizabeth Isabella Broughton, about seven years old. *Richard Read, 1814.*
This painting of Betsey was commissioned as a thank-you gift for the family who treated her so kindly during her year in Lima. The painting was eventually rediscovered in a second-hand shop in London in the 1950s.
T2707. BY PERMISSION OF THE NATIONAL LIBRARY OF AUSTRALIA.

Below: The Blowing Up of the **Boyd**. *Louis John Steele and Kennett Watkins, 1889.*
B.042363, MUSEUM OF NEW ZEALAND TE PAPA TONGAREWA, WELLINGTON.

Top: **The First Government Settlement on the Waitemata River, 1st October, 1840.** *John Johnson.* **This scene is exactly as described by Sarah in her memoirs.**
E-216-F-115, ALEXANDER TURNBULL LIBRARY, WELLINGTON.

Bottom: **The British flag first hoisted on the shores of the Waitemata, 18 September, 1840.** *John Johnson.* **Sarah can be clearly seen in bonnet and crinolined dress, the only European woman to be present on this occasion.**
HOCKEN LIBRARY, UARE TAOKA O HAKENA, UNIVERSITY OF OTAGO, DUNEDIN.

Top: Detail from 'Crossing the Teremakau'. *Nicholas Chevalier, 1876.*
B.041406. MUSEUM OF NEW ZEALAND TE PAPA TONGAREWA. WELLINGTON.

Bottom: The performance played on board HMS *Galatea*. *Nicholas Chevalier, 1866.*
B.038197, MUSEUM OF NEW ZEALAND TE PAPA TONGAREWA, WELLINGTON.

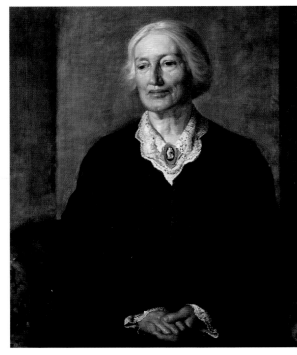

Left: **Portrait of Miss D. K. Richmond.** *H. Linley Richardson, c. 1924.*
B.041423, MUSEUM OF NEW ZEALAND
TE PAPA TONGAREWA, WELLINGTON.

Below: **'Passing time on board. Bertha is diligently knitting.'** *Mary Dobie, 1877.*
REPRODUCED BY COURTESY OF
MARGARET DRAKE BROCKMAN.

During Betsey's absence her father remarried, probably as much out of necessity as of love. Although his three oldest children were still living in England, William had his daughter Rebecca to care for and a home to run. William was well paid by colonial standards and, even with the prospect of stepchildren to rear, probably constituted quite a 'catch' for a young widow.

On 4 December 1810, just over a year from the time his beloved Elizabeth met her untimely death, William wed another Elizabeth. Elizabeth Charlotte was an Englishwoman, daughter of James Kennedy of Nettlestead, Kent, and widow of Captain Roger Simpson of Parramatta.

The *Atlanta* docked in Sydney at the end of May 1812 – Betsey's return home was some two and a half years after her departure from Sydney in the *Boyd*. The two-year-old toddler that William Broughton would have remembered was now almost five years old. He writes of 'the great joy of her disconsolate Father' but it must have been a confusing, possibly traumatic, homecoming for Betsey. Her last experience of a warm loving family had been the eleven months she had spent with the Ricos in Lima. Any recollection of her father and sister, Rebecca, would have been hazy in the extreme.

Berry's memoirs indicate that the return to Australia was, initially at least, difficult for Betsey. He notes: 'The girl herself [Betsey] would have been much pleased to have been left with her handsome mamma [Mrs Rico], and I was told by a lady in Sydney that she wished I had left her in Lima, and for that reason she never once paid me a visit when she came to Sydney.'

One way or another, Betsey had no option but to settle back into Broughton family life. Unlike her older siblings, she does not seem to have been sent to England for her education. This may reflect an increased number of educational options around Sydney, or perhaps stemmed from her father's fear of sending his precious daughter away again.

William's second marriage was a fruitful one with another five children added to the Broughton family. However, the couple had just eleven years together. William died on 22 July 1821, at the age of 53, while his wife Elizabeth remained on their farm, Lachlan Vale, Appin, until her death on 20 December 1843.

The *Dictionary of Australian Biography* notes that 'among a motley crowd of dissolute officials Broughton stands out as a loyal, trustworthy public servant, who, as Macquarie reported, performed "faithful, honest, useful and arduous Service" for thirty years; but because he had no powerful patron in London, he was consistently passed over in favour of less competent men.'

In 1822 Betsey's older sister Sarah was married to Charles Throsby Smith, nephew of William's great friends, Charles and Jane Throsby. Then, in 1824, the Throsby-Broughton family ties were further strengthened by the marriage of seventeen-year-old Betsey to another nephew, also named Charles Throsby. Charles senior was already a wealthy landowner in New South Wales and his nephew had recently arrived in the colony with the prospect of being his heir. The younger Charles Throsby also received grants totalling 2000 acres from the government. Betsey had made a good match by any colonial standard, with never a mention made of her mother's convict past.

In the manner of other landowners of the time the Throsbys farmed their land and ran their house with the assistance of 'assigned men and women', otherwise known as convict labour. The Throsbys had a reputation of being excellent employers who treated their workers well.

In the early years of their marriage Charles and Betsey lived in a colonial cottage – cosy to start with, but distinctly cramped by the time they'd produced their first six children. In 1834 work began on Throsby Park, a home more suited not only to the family's needs, but also to their status in the colony. In the manner of the day this was built with penal labour, taking 200 convicts three years to complete. In April 1837 William Walker, author of *A Month in the Bush in Australia*, wrote that the Throsbys' fine mansion 'was just finished and we stayed to dinner having being hospitably pressed to do so by Mr and Mrs Throsby'.

Once complete, the new house sheltered a sizeable household. The 1841 census shows that a total of forty-seven people were living at Throsby Park. In the house were one landed proprietor, five domestic servants and seven other persons (presumably Betsey and her six youngest children).

One of the most interesting, and interested, of many visitors to Throsby Park was Betsey's saviour at the time of the massacre, Alexander Berry. In 1838 he was travelling around the countryside with his wife, visiting friends as they went. He writes to a relative in London:

On our homeward journey we visited Throsby Park, the residence of Charles Throsby the husband of one of the children saved at New Zealand after the capture of the *Boyd*. Mr Throsby has a spacious and comfortable residence and is one of our rich Australian settlers. You may think it curious that Mrs Berry never saw this lady before – I saved her life as a child. She is now surrounded by a large family of children, and I may almost be considered as the constructive grandfather of the little imps.

The Throsby family was certainly large, and steadily growing. At this time Betsey was pregnant with her eighth child – her daughter Mary was born just two months after the Berrys' visit. In all, she had seventeen children, the first born when she was eighteen, the last at the age of forty-five.

Sadly, the following years brought a succession of tragedies to the Throsby household. In 1848 the second son died in a riding accident, followed soon after by nineteen-year-old William's death from scarlet fever. A third son, a baby of only three months, died in 1850, the only one of the Throsby children not to reach maturity.

In 1854 Charles Throsby died from a stroke, aged only fifty-four years. He was reputed to have been a very fine man – Alexander Berry describes him as 'active and manly', about the only personal comment that can be found about him. Charles had received a good start in the colony from his uncle, but never rested on his laurels, striving ever to better himself and to establish a strong financial base for his large family. He also worked hard for the colony and contributed usefully to its development and administration.

Three more of Betsey's sons were to die tragically over the next few years; the graves of six of her sons lie in a row below their local church at Bong Bong. It is hardly surprising that as the years passed by Betsey turned increasingly to her religion, being noted for her kindness to those in need.

Fortunately Betsey's daughters were not so cursed – they lived healthy lives and all married well, three to naval men. Those who lived close enough to their mother returned home to have their babies, suggesting a close relationship with their mother. These girls were by no means all society beauties. When one visitor was presented to the yet-unmarried Throsby girls he commented that one of them was 'a pretty pleasant looking young being – the other two very plain'.

In 1868 Betsey returned to live in the small, weatherboard cottage in which she had begun her married life. Now aged sixty-one, she was described

as 'the wealthy widow Mrs Throsby who prefers to occupy a pretty little sub-stantial cottage' with a view 'taking in a pond surrounded by weeping willows'.

Until a few months before her death, Betsey was 'often seen, driving through the town, or occupying a seat at her liberally endowed and cherished church at Bong Bong'. When, in January 1891, five-year-old Patrick Throsby wrote (with some help from his father) that 'poor Granny Throsby is no bet-ter and wanders in her mind a great deal of the time' Betsey only had a matter of days to live. She died, aged eighty-four, on 14 January.

The local paper, the *Scrutineer*, devoted a long article to Betsey's funeral. The service was conducted by three clergymen and the funeral cortège was exceptional; over fifty vehicles took part along with twenty horsemen. At the time of her death Betsey had seventy-eight grandchildren and eighteen great-grandchildren, many of whom would have attended, along with large numbers of friends and neighbours.

Daughter of a convict and survivor of a horrendous massacre, Betsey Broughton was always something of a legend in the colony. A lady by upbring-ing and marriage, if not by birth, this wealthy matriarch would have been quietly amused when the *Scrutineer* reported that her death had cast gloom over the Bong Bong Picnic Races. Several horses were scratched by their grief-struck owners, and only 150 people attended the event on the Club's 'picturesque course'.

POSTSCRIPT

In the 1950s, New Zealand art dealer and collector, Rex Nan Kivell, bought a por-trait of a young girl dressed in nineteenth-century costume from a second-hand shop in England. Once home he found a letter concealed inside the frame. The let-ter carried the inscription 'Elizabeth Isabella Broughton the subject of this portrait is the daughter of William Broughton Esq. Deputy Assistant Commissary General and one of his Majesty's Justices of the Peace for the Colony of New South Wales'. Then there is an account of Betsey's adventures until she returned home 'about the latter end of May 1812 to the great joy of her disconsolate Father who most respectfully inscribes this portrait to Don Gaspardo Rico and the other Spanish Gentlemen and Ladies as a tribute of respect and grateful remembrance'.

Elizabeth (Betsey) Throsby as an old lady. *F. Christo.*

A note at the bottom of the letter, written by the viceregal secretary, J.T. Campbell, stated that Governor Macquarie requested that Lord Strangford 'would use his endeavours' to forward the portrait to Lima. It is unknown what happened to the painting during the next 150 years, but it is now in the Australian National Library in Canberra.

The painting is by Richard Read who arrived in New South Wales in 1814.

Throsby Park Historic Site is managed by the NSW National Parks and Wildlife Service, and is one of the few historic homesteads within a day's drive of Sydney illustrating the activities of early colonial landholders. Built in 1834 on land granted by Governer Macquarie in 1819, this large and distinctive property was the home of the Throsby family for five generations. Open by arrangement for group bookings (phone 4887 7270).

BIBLIOGRAPHY

Australian Dictionary of Biography. Vol. 1, p. 157. Melbourne: Melbourne University Press, 1966.

Belich, James. *Making Peoples.* Auckland: Allen Lane, The Penguin Press, 1996.

Berry, Alexander. 'Account of the destruction of the ship Boyd and massacre of the Captain and crew, by the natives of Wangaroa New Zealand.' QMS-0163, Alexander Turnbull Library.

Berry, Alexander. *Reminiscences of Alexander Berry.* Sydney: Angus and Robertson, 1912.

Doak, Wade. *The Burning of the 'Boyd'.* *A Saga of Culture Clash.* Auckland: Hodder and Stoughton, 1984.

Howlett, Lorna. *The Throsbys of Throsby Park.* Published in Australia by Del Throsby, 1991.

Roxburgh, Rachel. *Throsby Park.* NSW National Parks and Wildlife Service, 1989.

Salmond, Anne. *Between Worlds.* Auckland: Viking/Penguin, 1997.

SARAH MATHEW
C. 1805 – 1890

SOCIAL COMMENTATOR

THE NOISE AND CONFUSION WAS ABSOLUTELY DEAFENING ... THE WEATHER WAS SO BAD ALL THIS DAY ... I NEVER WAS IN A VESSEL THAT ROLLED SO TREMENDOUSLY AS SHE DOES. I WAS TWICE FORCIBLY EJECTED from my bed and only escaped being very much hurt by throwing my feet first and, so alighting on them, instead of my head ... It was without exception the most terrible day I ever spent at sea ...

Three days of utter misery follow, which makes a blank in my journal ... Dr. Johnson, however, insisted on my trying to walk a little this evening, and with his assistance I managed to do so for a short time, but I am very weak and often feel like fainting, which last is a new accomplishment for me ...

The wind today still contrary, with showers and cold, disagreeable weather; I, however, kept on deck as long as possible, feeling so much worse when below ... I was obliged to retire to my cabin, where I passed

Sarah Mathew, 1845.

THE FOUNDING OF NEW ZEALAND, ED J. RUTHERFORD, REED, 1940.

a miserable night, alternately sick and tossed almost out of my bed with the violent rolling and pitching of the vessel ...

Despite the discomfort, Sarah is a dutiful diarist, resolutely cheerful and ever-fascinated by her fellow travellers and the shipboard doings. A warm-hearted woman, she quickly makes friends with others of her station and tantalises us with some cryptic comments:

> In the course of this day all my companions have come on board; one or two among them I think will prove valuable acquaintances. I am quite prepossessed in Mrs Freeman's favour; I begin to think and hope that she has been cruelly calumniated; it is hard to believe that depravity can lurk under so sweet, and simple, and gentle an exterior ...

Just the description to whet our appetites for gossip about honour compromised, reputations ruined and scandalous tales of illicit passion. Sadly, Sarah does nothing to enlighten us, but, quite charmed by the lady, she is uncharacteristically and frustratingly discreet:

> ... She is extremely fascinating; her manners so quiet, so artless, and so winning, that it is impossible to believe that she can ever have erred beyond perhaps some imprudences which, considering her youth, are almost pardonable. She appears to be much younger than I had thought her, she can scarcely be more than twenty ...

Further acquaintance only serves to increase the attraction, albeit somewhat qualified:

> Mrs Freeman is a woman of cultivated mind and talents, I think ill-directed; she reads Latin authors with apparent pleasure and writes very passable poetry with ease. She read me yesterday some pretty lines she had composed, which I criticised unmercifully ... The only thing I do not like about her is a sort of perpetual representation as it seems ... her every action and every attitude is a picture, and I cannot yet satisfy myself whether all her grace, simplicity and innocence and artlessness

is not in fact most exquisite acting …

Then, there's Mrs Burrowes, 'a most agreeable person, one whom, you may at once feel, it is allowable to like without hesitation. She is a quiet, lady-like person, very preferable in my opinion, to her husband.'

During this two-week voyage days are whiled away in a companionable manner. Diaries are written, whist is played. Mrs Freeman and Sarah have their mattresses always side by side and happily spend long hours in discussion of French writers and general chat. The charming Mrs Burrowes sits with them and does her 'work' and the good Dr Johnson joins in their discussions:

> We form a very pleasant little coterie … Mrs Freeman, who enjoys excellent spirits, strove to amuse me and Dr Johnson with her wild Welsh Melodies … she has a rich, splendid voice, but totally uncultivated, and she seems quite ignorant of the power she possesses.

There are upsets, of course. Sarah and her fellow cabin passengers[1] were disturbed by a minor revolt among the deck passengers when 'a hard, stern-looking Highlander … most violent in his manner and language … a stonemason [with] a very sinister appearance' refused to hand water out of the hold for the horses. He was clapped in irons and placed under the care of an armed sentry, his screaming wife and children firmly dispatched back down below.

Although Sarah concedes that the emigrants below decks may have something to complain about ('they are very poorly supplied with provisions, some are almost starving, and that naturally makes them discontented') that is as far as her concern extends. She writes with feeling that those below decks must 'be one and all the very worst of their class that could possibly be selected, and the noise and confusion with the screaming and scolding of the women and children is enough to try the patience of a meeker man than our captain'.

In marked contrast to many of the missionaries she later scorned, Sarah was always conscious of her social place, displaying little or no sympathy for the less privileged. Seventeen years previously, in 1823, Marianne Williams,

---

[1] Deck or steerage passengers were emigrants travelling in generally communal conditions with the most basic of amenities. Cabin or First Class passengers such as Sarah Mathew were much better off – they had their own cabins and had their food cooked and served to them as if in a good hotel.

the wife of missionary Henry Williams, had spent much of her seagoing time in the appalling conditions below decks, doing her best to improve the lot of convict and free women alike. You would never have found Sarah there. However, Sarah's attitudes were probably entirely typical of most of her contemporaries – she was very much a product of the age. Selfless missionaries are much more likely to have been the exception, as removed from their European compatriots as most twentieth-century women were from Mother Theresa.

It is probably true that Sarah experienced more heartfelt concern for the horses on board than for the people below decks. Many of the unfortunate beasts suffered badly in the stormy conditions with much damage being done. Sarah was most relieved to find that her 'poor beauty was fortunately on the weather side and is, I am told, quite well and saucy'.

Seasickness was an ongoing problem for Sarah, and Mrs Burrowes had a 'terrible fall' that created concern for her 'very delicate situation'. All rallied around and the good doctor dosed her liberally with red lavender drops, port wine and water – a brew potently topped up with a generous measure of laudanum. It is hardly surprising that she was reported as sleeping quietly, and she recovered well within two days.

A London lass, Sarah Louise Mathew was probably born in 1805 – no record of her birth has been traced, but she was christened on 19 November of that year. Although her father's occupation is unclear, we do know that the family moved in educated and literary circles. One of her four siblings, George Felton Mathew, was later a great friend of John Keats.

Highly intelligent and with a strong literary inclination, at fifteen years old Sarah avidly read books on history, travel, adventure and poetry, admitting to a particular love for Shakespeare, Milton, Scott, Rogers, Campbell and 'Mason on Self-Knowledge'. Sarah was fortunate in receiving an education that was exceptionally broad for a girl of her times as, although she came from a 'good family', it was not a wealthy one. There was never any doubt that Sarah would have to make her own way in the world.

In 1822 Sarah started work as a governess, one of the few careers open to a well-educated, respectable woman. Her first position was with a military family, looking after the children of Lieutenant Colonel Cameron, 79th Regiment, at Millbrook, Southampton and later at Beverley in the north of England. Further engagements were with families at Nottingham and Tunbridge Wells.

We know little of the life Sarah led, but there were obviously strong ties with, and affection for, other branches of the family. In 1829 Sarah became engaged to her cousin, Felton Mathew, her elder by four years. Their troth plighted, Felton set sail for Australia to take up a position as assistant surveyor of roads and bridges in Sydney. Sarah wrote later that 'his ambition and desire to be useful induced him to go abroad, though he preferred England'. Two years later, in 1831, when Sarah would have been about twenty-six, she travelled to New South Wales to marry her cousin.

Unfortunately no letters have been traced from this time. It was a remarkable act of faith for any young woman in the 1830s to set sail to unknown lands to marry her beloved. At that time ships often took five months to complete the journey – communications during the lovers' two-year separation must have been sketchy in the extreme, any protestations of love or reassurances of future domestic bliss ages old before Sarah even boarded her ship. It might have taken half a year for Felton's latest love letters to reach Sarah – fervent words perhaps already regretted, but certainly her last word from him for perhaps the next six months while she packed her bags, secured a passage and sailed for southern seas. By the time Felton and Sarah were reunited on the Sydney dockside, a full year could easily have passed since they last communicated – unnerving by any modern lovers' standards.

However, all was apparently well and Sarah and Felton were married in Sydney on 21 January 1832. For the next eight years the Mathews lived at Windsor, on the Hawkesbury River, thirty-five miles from Sydney. Felton was appointed town surveyor in 1835, and soon afterwards was offered the post of Chief Surveyor at Port Phillip. A cautious man, he declined the post as he considered that such a colonial government appointment was rather less secure than one made by Downing Street. It was an unfortunate decision: in 1839 changes were made so the colony could have more power in the management of its affairs and Felton's post was abolished.

Fortunately, Captain Hobson, prospective Governor of New Zealand, sailed in to Felton's rescue, offering him the position of acting Surveyor-General in New Zealand. With little option but to accept, Felton travelled to New Zealand on HMS *Herald* in January 1840, apparently under the impression that his appointment would be confirmed in England. Somewhat bitter about the whole business, the self-important Felton writes in his first letter to Sarah that he holds 'no faith with the scoundrel Government which has used us so vilely, but to make use of them for our own purposes and throw them off as soon as it suits our convenience'.

Sarah stayed a little longer in Sydney, arranging the shipment of equipment and their household belongings. Her detailed diaries of shipboard life and travels with her husband began when she boarded the New Zealand-bound *Westminster* on 2 March 1840.

The strength of the Mathews' relationship is very apparent in the letters and diaries written during their months apart. During the weeks of waiting for Sarah to arrive in New Zealand, Felton writes to his beloved wife ever fondly: 'Would you were here dearest to talk this matter over … I am eagerly looking out every hour for your arrival.' And when he is getting truly demoralised by personal disputes and petty politics he writes: 'The *Westminster* is coming along the Coast. If you were not in her, mine own, I should feel strongly inclined to "give up everything" and return to Sydney forthwith.'

Sarah appears equally devoted to Felton, stalwartly overcoming her limitations as a traveller to be with him at every opportunity. Arriving in the Bay of Islands, she reports with the greatest of enthusiasm: 'Several boats were seen approaching and in one of them I had the supreme delight of seeing my precious husband.' On a later journey, when accompanying Felton on the trip to purchase the site for the new capital of Auckland, Sarah feels a little dispirited as the barque *Anna Watson* prepares to set sail. This is not a journey she would ever have contemplated without her beloved husband:

> I am the only lady and my position is not an enviable one; it is true I have the comfort of my husband's company and a precious privilege it is to be his companion everywhere; but I suffer so much on board ship, and my health is so indifferent that I set out on this voyage with a very heavy heart.

Although Sarah became pregnant on a number of occasions, all her babies miscarried or were stillborn. Writing from Paihia in July 1840, when she was about thirty-five years old, she sadly notes: 'I do not expect it at all now, I am too old, and have had too many mishaps. I do not much mind but I fancy Felton thinks more about [it] since the last 2 I lost. They were such pretty little creatures, he buried them both in our garden at … and when we left it there was a beautiful weeping willow growing over them.'

However, in later letters and diaries there is neither mention of past sadness, nor any hint of ongoing grief as a result of their childlessness – the Mathews were of sterling pioneer stock, determinedly and (generally) cheerfully moving on to their next challenges. Certainly their marital relationship was a devoted one; there is no doubt that they were the best of friends, the closest of confidants.

A less intrepid woman would have quietly made a base at Paihia and dutifully waited for her husband to return between surveying trips. Nothing so tame for the indomitable Sarah, brought up as she was on tales of travel, adventure and romance. Sarah sailed with Felton at every opportunity, facing very difficult conditions as she toured the coast with him in the little cutter *Ranger*, sleeping in tents or open boats in the autumn and winter chill, scrambling through bush and over hills, copying Felton's reports at aching length. Her lack of children gave her the option to be 'a camp follower', but it was never an easy path, and one probably looked at askance by other ladies in the colony.

Sarah's loyalty is particularly admirable given that Felton could be difficult. Always extremely self-important, he was a fussy little man, very aware of his personal dignity and that of his office. Felton was easily affronted, continually on the lookout for anything that could possibly be construed as a slight. A sense of humour is never apparent in his writing.

Lady Franklin, wife of Sir John Franklin, Governor of Van Diemen's Land, visited Auckland in 1841 and judged Felton to be an 'important little personage, highly disputable in character, clever as a public official, but excessively vain'. In contrast, Lady Franklin considered Mrs Felton Mathew to be 'an amiable woman'.

There is also a measure of suspicion that Felton was involved in some early shady land dealings when options for establishing the capital in the Bay of Islands were being considered. Whatever the case, his letters are fascinating as he confides matters of great import to Sarah:

We have had such an explosion this morning between the two Captains, who are both obstinate, wrong-headed fellows … The quarrel has been

Sarah Mathew on her horse Lucifer, 1832. *Artist unknown.*
Silhouette in black ink. From Mrs Mathew's scrapbook.
AUCKLAND PUBLIC LIBRARY.

very violent ... Captain Nias has certainly shewn great want of feeling,
and much indelicacy in wishing to hurry Hobson out of the ship: but the
latter ... is a most disagreeable person to have anything to do with ...
Hobson is no more fit for the duty he has undertaken than I am to be Lord
Chancellor ...

Unlike her husband, Sarah, combined a strong intellect with charm, warmth
and evident humour. She could be exceptionally critical in what she wrote
about others, but her words were written for her and Felton alone – her
journals were never intended for publication. It is obvious that when Sarah
liked people she warmed to them greatly and was generous in her praise when
the occasion and the person merited it. When she and Felton finally left the
Westminster Sarah wrote of the 'kind, liberal Captain' in the most glowing of
terms. 'We shall be delighted to see him again in any quarter of the world.'

At other times the unashamedly sharp-penned Sarah was rather less complimentary. She reports Marianne Williams to be 'a plain sort of motherly woman' with 'a large family of raw, uncouth boys and girls', an impression which appears kindly when compared with her blistering comments on other inhabitants of the Bay of Islands. Her opinion appears not to have been shared by other guests and is likely to have been unduly harsh. However, Sarah is impressed by Henry Williams, 'a man of rather prepossessing manners and far superior to any of the missionaries I have seen'.

A devoted Christian, the miserably seasick Sarah insisted on reading Sunday service even when the sea was too rough for shipboard services. Once in New Zealand, just getting to church could be a formidable challenge – the Mathews came in from the ship, a trip that involved landing at Paihia in the rolling surf. Their 'Sunday best' must have been distinctly damp by the time they walked in the door. Once there, the music from the barrel organ was found most satisfactory, but the minister was not. Missionaries seldom found favour with Sarah's brutally blunt pen:

> The service was performed by Mr Burrowes, whom I like less than ever, for being no longer strictly confined to the rules and customs of our liturgy, he launched forth in the usual whine and rant of dissenters in general, and both before and after a tolerable sermon, he gave us an extemporaneous effusion of the greatest nonsense possible.

Another service, two weeks later, brought her no more joy.

> Went to church at Paihia, heard Mr Wilson perform the service. He is the most doleful, whining, miserable creature imaginable; quite dismal enough to make anyone afraid of the religion he pretends to teach.

And it wasn't just the missionaries who got the rough side of Sarah's pen. Her shipboard friend, the amiable Mrs Burrowes, was staying with her sister Mrs Ford. Sarah was unimpressed: 'I do not like Mrs Ford at all; she is very inferior to her sister, and the whole aspect of the place seemed dirty and uncomfortable … The weather cleared off in the afternoon, and being much disgusted with the Fords, we soon returned to the ship.'

Although Sarah is much kinder about the wife of the American Consul,

Captain Clendon, her praise is tempered by critical comment. When Sarah writes of the Clendons' great kindness and hospitality she elaborates:

> Mrs Clendon seems a very kind sort of good creature, and has a numerous family, but I cannot say much for her refinement or education; yet she has all the comforts and many of the luxuries of civilised life about her, the house is very neatly finished and seems well furnished, there is a splendid piano by Broadwood in the drawing room, but so woefully out of tune that it is quite impossible to touch it. We drank tea from splendid china served on a silver salver, and about 9 o'clock took leave of our kind hostess, whose trouble with her guests was much increased by a cross, screaming babe of 4 months old.

Although Sarah certainly did not enjoy the rigours of ocean travel, she revelled in smaller trips, in and around the settlements.

> Captain Clendon took us down to our boat, and we pulled off by the light of a beautiful moon, and enjoyed a most delightful row. Mrs Freeman sang my favourite melody most exquisitely, and afterwards two very beautiful duets with her husband.

Sarah loved the magnificent outdoor environment of this new land: her elegant descriptions of scenes and events are consistently enthusiastic. The party dined alfresco at the new flagstaff in honour of Mrs Freeman's birthday, building a large fire 'piled with huge trees' to warm the occasion. It was a late return to the ship: 'The waters were beautifully phosphorescent, splashing like liquid silver with every dip of the oars. On the way a guardfish jumped into the boat and was retained … for the morning's breakfast.'

Sarah generally admired the scenery more than those who inhabited it. At Russell (Kororareka) Europeans and Maori alike failed to impress.

> The store was surrounded with a motley assembly of natives – men, women and children, and such a set of Europeans I never beheld. Some, who from birth and education should have been gentlemen, no longer presented the slightest trace of having ever seen civilised life; a sort of reckless vulgarity

and impudence characterised them all and I was glad to transact my business and get away from such a scene of noise and confusion.

Sarah's comments on local Maori are of particular interest. Her initial assumption of superiority meant that she was distinctly unsettled by the visit of King and Queen Pomare. Unnervingly, she found the social positions she expected reversed – to her bemused surprise the visitors appeared to be treating her with condescension. Distinctly affronted, Sarah didn't mince words as to what she thought of the regal pair:

> Mrs Clendon came to call on me and brought King and Queen Pomaree and all their court to see me. She advised me to receive them with much consideration as Pomaree was a very powerful chief and had much influence among his people, so I of course made myself as amiable as possible though much disgusted with the odious savages. They seemed so conceited and so perfectly indifferent, almost contemptuous, in their manner towards us, as if they were really conferring an honour by their visit – a set of dirty disgusting savages.

Sarah later notes that Henry Williams had given them a letter to the chiefs of the tribes near Thames 'which I hope will be of use to us in case of any hostile collision with any of the natives in that neighbourhood; it seems they are in a rather disturbed state at present and do not seem quite to understand the terms on which we have entered the country'. With advice like that, travel was hardly for the faint-hearted. Given the warlike appearance of many local Maori and the unsettled mood in the country, it was exceptionally brave of Sarah to consider venturing out into the unknown on Felton's surveying expeditions.

On 6 April 1840 Felton was instructed to proceed south in the revenue cutter *Ranger* in order to select a site for the chief settlement and government of the colony. On Saturday 18 April Felton and Sarah boarded the cutter. Although there was little wind, Sarah 'soon became sick and sad and went to bed'. The next day was worse, but on the Monday they anchored in 'Wangari' [Whangarei] Bay, a spot so beautiful that Sarah found it distinctly therapeutic:

I was perfectly delighted and lost almost all sense of sea-sickness in the bold magnificent scenery it presented; such lofty craggy heights I never saw, the sides of them generally covered with trees and beautifully green; the summits were broken into pinnacles and masses of rocks resembling towers and walls and bastions; indeed very little help of the imagination might transfer the scene to the banks of the Rhine.

The seas were bountiful. The crew were busy 'pulling up the fish as fast as the hooks were thrown; very fine fish they are – schnappers, gurnet and what is called salmon in these seas'.

Occasional meetings with other Europeans occurred, including several white men:

> ... a strange set of beings, settlers from the Thames and Coromandel Harbour – and such specimens of settlers; many degrees below those of New South Wales in apparent respectability. Truly the early settlers in a new colony do become most extraordinary beings, somewhat I imagine of the Kentucky style 'half horse, half alligator, with a touch of the earth-quake'.

These extraordinary beings were almost definitely founding father of Auckland, John Logan Campbell and his friends Webster and Brown. Undoubtedly interesting, but not half as colourful as those the Mathews met some four weeks later, when they arrived at Coromandel. Landing at Webster's house, they sat down to dinner with some other guests:

> ... adventurers of all kinds, from the honourable (quasi) Dudley Sinclair, member of the Port Nicholson Assembly, to the half piratical master of several vessels strongly suspected of being concerned in the slave trade ... there were a few natives about; one of them, a very fine looking old man, was pointed out to me as having seen our great navigator Captain Cook. He described the wonder of his countrymen on the approach of Captain Cook's boat.

On Tuesday 5 May they explored a volcanic island opposite the mouth of the

Volcanic hills in the vicinity of Auckland. *Felton Mathew, c. 1845.*
E-389-Q-010, ALEXANDER TURNBULL LIBRARY, WELLINGTON.

'Tehmaki' [Tamaki] river and then, after dinner, set off to explore the hills of the mainland. This appealed to Sarah greatly – she could quite envisage herself living there:

> It is very fatiguing to scramble among these hills, for the loose stones roll beneath the feet and the fern and brushwood is so thick you cannot see your footpath. It is, however, a very beautiful spot and might be made still more beautiful by cultivation. I had many pleasing daydreams here. I pictured my cottage in some sheltered knoll, its beautiful garden full of flowers and redolent of scents; my romantic walks among the hills or on the sands; the really magnificent sea view presented on every side forming the background to every such picture.

Sarah must have been remarkably fit, apparently easily keeping up with Felton despite the hindrance of her ladylike, but entirely impractical,

53

garments. One day, exploring up the Tehmaki, they travelled up the river for ten miles, rowed (well, at least the men rowed) for another two hours, and then walked for two hours to gain a view of the 'Manakao' [Manukau] Harbour.

> At first our walk was difficult and painful, for though thickly covered with fern and brush the surface of the ground was so rugged and strewn with large masses of volcanic stone that almost every step was a stumble … in about two hours we reached the top of the hill … we managed to climb the remainder by clinging to the branches and fern, without much difficulty.

Walking was made easier on those days that they set fire to the fern on their way up a hill. 'By following the course which our fire had cleared we returned to our boat with little difficulty, the walking through blackened stems of fern and brush being a trifle compared with our usual scrambling.' Sarah's fine dresses must have suffered badly when landing variously in rolling surf or mud-flats, bushwhacking and trailblazing, her long skirts often sweeping across newly burned fernland. Of a later ascent of Rangitoto, Sarah comments: 'The sharp rocks and scoria had worn my boots to pieces, and my dress of grey merino was torn in shreds, struggling through the thorny brush wood, and by the sharp edges of the rocks.' That note apart, however, never a mention is made of problems with clothes during this adventurous period and the issue of laundry is never addressed.

In September of 1840 Felton and Sarah Mathew were members of the expedition that set out to proclaim Auckland as the capital of New Zealand. Strong interpersonal tensions within the party made this a difficult journey for Sarah. The older officers greatly resented the appointment of Captain Symonds as head of the expedition and the hugely affronted Felton actually tendered his resignation at one point: '… I do not think proper to place myself in a position which is calculated to degrade my office within the eyes of others. I … request that immediate steps may be taken for relieving me from my duties.'

This resignation was not accepted, but relationships were inevitably some-what strained. To make matters worse, the ship, the *Anna Watson*, was badly maintained. Sarah writes:

I do not find my position here very pleasant; the Captain is too good-natured, he suffers so much disorder and discomfort to prevail without any effort to remedy it that I am much disappointed. The ship though such a fine sailing vessel and so admirably arranged as to comfort, is rendered by neglect and dirt a most uncomfortable abode …

Things were looking a little better the following day. Friday, 18 September 1840 was the chosen day for signing the preliminary agreement with Ngati Whatua leaders for the purchase of the site of Auckland. Sarah describes the scene:

A beautiful morning seemed to smile on the auspicious circumstance of taking formal possession of a certain portion of the land: and accordingly preparations were made for the important ceremony, and about half past twelve the whole party landed and proceeded to the height where the Flag staff was raised ready to receive the Royal Standard …

Then the flag was run up, and the whole assembly gave three cheers, the ship's colours were also instantly hoisted and a Salute of 21 guns fired. Her Majesty's health was then most rapturously drunk with cheers long and loud repeated from the ships … As it was wished to make this somewhat of a holiday the gentlemen got up a boat race among themselves, another for the sailors, and a canoe race for the natives, which all came off with great éclat.

Auckland proclaimed, Sarah at last saw hope of an end to her travelling life: 'If we remain I begin to flatter myself I may have again ere very long, something like a comfortable dwelling and a nice garden.' And with more confidence some two weeks later, 'I have been enclosing a small plot of ground for my bulbs which are all shooting and should be planted.'

Plans for domesticity received a significant setback when a scrub fire got out of control and burned its way to the Government Store. Much was destroyed including some of the Mathew possessions. Sarah laments: 'I shall suffer much inconvenience from the loss of the large case containing my stock of Ironmongery and the whole of my culinary apparatus. My dining tables have escaped with a slight scorching and the splitting of one of the leaves.' She then continues in stoic vein: 'I am thankful that no lives have been lost, and the damage sustained no greater.'

Two days later they gladly took leave of the *Anna Watson*, ('a more dirty ill conditioned vessel I never had the misfortune to be in') and took up residence on the shore.

> Our whole property is piled up beside our tent and covered from the weather by a Tarpaulin. Our tent is sheltered by a coppice and open only towards the sea, and is really very comfortable considering … There is a beautiful stream running through the centre of the little amphitheatre or valley, and the landscape is really a gem.

This may have been idyllic to look at, but it was less than ideal when the Mathews wanted to take a quiet stroll. 'There is a Maori path winding through the copse up the hill to the Flag staff, and thus far is our usual evening walk, the whole country is covered with Fern that it is difficult to move in any other direction. The only mode of clearing it is by burning, and then to walk over the blackened ground is destructive to dress.' This doesn't sound like the earlier travel journals when no conditions provided too much of a challenge – bushwhacking clothes had obviously been dispensed with, the intrepid exploring Sarah quietly replaced by a lady of breeding who dressed according to her station and 'kept up appearances'!

Shelter for the horses was a priority – even before their tents were pitched Felton and Sarah 'got some natives to make a "warre" [whare or native hut] for our horses which were still on board the Ship … My poor beauty, how glad he was to get on shore; and what lovely rides I had over the country, mostly all covered with fern, or low bushes and only traversed by native paths.'

Sarah not only ran the household with the assistance of her twelve-year-old servant, Helen, but also helped Felton compile his detailed reports. Sarah's social presence and skill as a hostess were indisputably of immeasurable value to Felton. The fact that the Governor appears to have treated their tent as a second home, dining there with happy frequency whenever he visited Auckland, implies that Felton must have got over his early antipathy for Hobson. Sarah writes that Hobson made their tent 'his home, his Office and

Government House, Auckland. *Edward Ashworth, 1842 or 1843.*
E-216-F-005, ALEXANDER TURNBULL LIBRARY, WELLINGTON.

everything else'. Sarah was sure to have been the social facilitator, only too competent at pouring oil on troubled waters. When in March 1841 Governor and Mrs Hobson finally did move to the still-uncompleted Government House in Auckland the Mathews were frequent visitors.

This Government House sounded much grander than it really was. In 1843 Mrs Fitzroy, wife of the newly appointed Governor, succinctly described it as 'a barn divided into unpapered and unpainted rooms'. She certainly wouldn't have mourned when this first Government House was destroyed by fire in 1848. It was replaced by the 'Old Government House' that stands to this day in the grounds of Auckland University.

We gain a more detailed insight into the practicalities of life in early Auckland from Sarah's autobiography, written some 30 years later. Food was an ongoing challenge, especially when the Governor was a regular dinner guest. Shops were still non-existent, but the resourceful Sarah

> … had a supply of Preserved meats and soups, and the natives would per-
> haps bring some fish, if I bribed them with a present of tobacco or flour or
> sugar … We used to bake cakes in a camp oven … We had at that time
> plenty of wood, which the Natives used to bring in huge loads on their

backs, as well as potatoes and Kumeras, which they gladly sold to us for 6d. or 1/- according to size.

We used to buy Stores from the Ships which came in; barrels of American flour, and biscuits, and dried apples, the latter exceedingly good; they are pared, cut in quarters, strung upon twine, and so after drying in the sun, or oven, are packed in casks. We used to buy them from the American Whaleships, which are always supplied with these apples, as they are found to be an excellent anti-scorbutic on long voyages. We used them for pudding and sauce for the Pork, which at first was the only fresh meat we could get; so we used to dress it in a variety of ways with seasoning to make it resemble beef, mutton, or veal ... Then if a Ship arrived from India or China, we used to get barrels of Sugar and bags of Rice, preserves and Tea in Chests ... I used to make my bread on the top of a cask outside the tent.

Mary Anne Martin, wife of New Zealand's first Chief Justice, William Martin, also wrote of food issues in Auckland at this time. She commented on the monotony of pork and how they sometimes removed its rind and served it up in the guise of boiled mutton with caper sauce and Swedish turnips – we're not told if anyone was convinced that it was anything but pork! Milk was entirely unobtainable, and butter a scarce and expensive luxury.

As for accommodation, Sarah writes:

After a time we got Natives to build us a regular native house of two rooms, with a roof of Palm leaves and Rapoo [raupo], or reed thatch over it ... The doors and window frames, we bought from an enterprising carpenter who made these things for sale, and for glass we had oiled calico, which kept out the rain and gave us light enough within, tho' of course no view.

This 'native house' must have served them for some time because it was not until the settlement's second year that 'the sale of the Allotments' took place. Official Bay at the east side of Point Britomart had been set aside for officials who had been allowed to select their land before any land sales took place. It

St Paul's Church and the Residence of Felton Mathew, Official Bay, 1845. *Felton Mathew.*
From Mrs Mathew's scrapbook.
AUCKLAND PUBLIC LIBRARY.

had been agreed that they would pay for their allotments after the first Land Sale – the price was to be whatever the average price at the sale had been.

The Mathews bought two allotments in Official Bay, including the 'pretty spot on which our tents first stood'. Shortly afterwards their house was built of Tasmanian hardwood.

> It cost upwards of £2000, though of very moderate dimensions and simple
> construction, much after the fashion of an Indian Bungalow, all on the
> ground floor, with windows to the ground opening on a wide Verandah,
> and a terrace, beyond which a sloping lawn with flower beds and then a
> belt of shrubbery partly native trees but sown with acorns, chestnuts, wal-
> nuts, and planted with vines and fig trees which we brought from Sydney.

St Paul's Church was built just behind their house.

Settled they may have been, but Sarah's travelling days were not yet over. Two years later the Mathews accompanied the Governor on a trip to Akaroa,

Barrett's Hotel, Wellington. *Samuel Charles Brees. 1847.*
A-109-027, ALEXANDER TURNBULL LIBRARY, WELLINGTON.

Wellington and other Cook Strait settlements. The French colony of Akaroa was a particular highlight, the French exceedingly hospitable and charming and Sarah in great demand as interpreter for the Governor. What's more, Sarah recounts, 'I was the only lady of the party, and of course was made a great deal of.'

Then there was Wellington:

A few scattered houses of wood, along the beach, contained the whole population. There was one of rather larger size than the rest, called an Hotel, and there rooms were taken for the Governor and his staff, and there we also found a room … The Superintendent, Colonel Wakefield, had a small but comfortable wooden house, and he gave some dinner parties to the Governor, to which we of course were invited.

Sarah's notes include a telling insight into Maori land issues. There was a grand 'Korero' when the chiefs of the principal tribes came to explain to the Governor that:

the Company had not paid for the land they had taken, and there was a great deal of discontent, and some hostility among them. There were Missionaries to interpret their Speeches, and some were very threatening and unpleasant, but they were soothed with fair words and presents of Flour and sugar and plenty of Tobacco.

Back in Auckland life and years rolled on with the infant colony gaining some vestiges of 'society'. The Governor and Mrs Hobson were well established at Government House and many other families also settled in the surrounding area. There were visits to pay, parties and balls. A Philharmonic Society was formed with monthly meetings regularly ending with a dance. Mary Anne Martin described the rigours of a Government House ball when bad weather made the roads almost impassable. Nobody gave up. One chivalrous husband conveyed his wife up to Government House in a wheelbarrow while less indulged ladies borrowed their partners' jackboots, tucked up their skirts and waded through the quagmire. Forget the rain – let the band begin!

Passing missionaries (hopefully more congenial than those of early acquaintance) would stay for a night or two. Then there was a flurry of marriages, held, in the absence of a church, at Government House. The weddings took place in the evenings, always followed by a ball at which the Governor would faithfully dance the first quadrille with the bride. Honeymoons were hardly practicable, so after the celebrations the bride would just walk to her new home, the groom appearing at his usual post in the morning.

Once Auckland was proclaimed as capital Felton, as Surveyor General, produced a controversial design for the city based on a plan of quadrants and crescents. His opponents, however, claimed that the design failed to take into account any irregularities of topography and it was therefore abandoned.

In 1845, frustrated at the lack of progress in confirming Felton either in his position of Surveyor General or as Chief Police Magistrate (he was acting in this role), the Mathews sailed to England in order to have the situation clarified. There was no happy resolution. Although the Mathews returned to New Zealand in March 1847 thinking they had succeeded in their mission, difficulties with the new Governor, George Grey, negated all they had done. Disappointed, they sold their house and possessions and sailed for England once more in September. Felton was stressed and unwell when they departed and became steadily worse, dying at Lima in Peru at the end of November.

Already disappointed that life in the colony had not turned out as they had hoped and worked so hard for, this must have been a devastating blow for the devoted Sarah. Few nineteenth-century couples would have shared such adventurous lives or seen so many matters of moment together. More than just a husband, Felton was undoubtedly Sarah's closest confidant and companion, the entire focus of her life – his death would have left her completely bereft.

Once back in England, Sarah settled near Seaford in Sussex. Bitter at the treatment Felton had received, in 1848 she applied to the British Government for compensation for injustices she believed Felton had suffered. This application was unsuccessful.

Ten years later, when Sarah was about fifty-three, she returned once more to Auckland hoping to resolve some issues of property. The intervening boom years had quietened and to her disappointment she found that, despite significant immigration, land was a difficult commodity to sell.

Sarah returned to England for the last time in 1861. Her autobiography dates from a decade later – a charming and highly informative account of life in early New Zealand which, along with her diaries and letters, gives a fascinating eye-witness account of New Zealand's colonial past.

Sarah died at Tonbridge, Kent, on 14 December 1890, a most respectable eighty-five years old.

BIBLIOGRAPHY

Belich, James. *Making Peoples.* Auckland: Allen Lane, The Penguin Press, 1996.

Dictionary of New Zealand Biography, Vol 1. Wellington: Bridget Williams Books, Department of Internal Affairs, p. 282.

Drummond, Alison. *Married and Gone to New Zealand.* New Zealand: Paul's Book Arcade, Hamilton and Auckland. London: Oxford University Press, 1961.

Mathew, F. & Mathew, S. *The Founding of New Zealand.* Ed. J. Rutherford. Dunedin: Published for the Auckland University College by A.H. & A.W. Reed, 1940.

Mathew, F. & Mathew, S. 'Journals, Letters and Sketch-books, 1840–1848.' MS. AP.

Moon, Paul. *Hobson, Governor of New Zealand, 1840–1842.* Auckland: David Ling Publishing, 1998.

Platts, U. *The Lively Capital, Auckland 1840–1865.* Christchurch: Avon Fine Prints Ltd, 1971.

Porter, Frances and MacDonald, Charlotte (Eds). *My Hand Will Write What My Heart Dictates.* Auckland: Auckland University Press, Bridget Williams Books, 1996.

The Shoot.
after passing the Hummu' Saddle

CAROLINE CHEVALIER
c. 1832 – 1917

ON HEARING WE WERE BOUND FOR HOKITIKA, SHE SIMPLY STOOD STILL, EYED ME UP AND DOWN WITH RATHER A SCORNFUL LOOK FOR I AM A LITTLE WOMAN AND NO DOUBT THEN BEING YOUNG LOOKED VERY insignificant. And she exclaimed 'You going to the West Coast. I am a good horse woman, but my husband would not think of taking me there. You know you've got to cross rivers aye and swim them.'

And it wasn't just this farmer's wife who doubted the wisdom of the young Caroline accompanying her husband over the Southern Alps to the West Coast and back again. Although Caroline's husband, artist Nicholas Chevalier, 'greatly desired me to accompany him ... friends thought it very risky. Indeed full of difficulties for a man, but impossible for a woman to ride 400 miles at least, and camp out and cross rivers and various minor difficulties.'

Reservations there may have been, but Caroline had an adventurous

'The shoot after passing the Hurunui Saddle.' *Attributed to Nicholas Chevalier, but, as with many of the sketches of this trip, may actually have been by Caroline. 1866.*
A-102-029, ALEXANDER TURNBULL LIBRARY, WELLINGTON.

65

spirit. 'I was young and had no fear. I was very enthusiastic and longed to go, come what might.'

This was by no means the first significant adventure in Caroline's life, though it did promise to be the most uncomfortable. An Englishwoman, London born and bred, Caroline was the daughter of noted amateur artist Frederick Wilkie and was reputed to be a competent artist herself. Art was not an isolated talent in this gifted family – Frederick's cousin was Sir David Wilkie, R.A., an eminent Scottish artist who had been appointed to the role of 'Painter to the King' in 1830.

We know little about the young Caroline's upbringing – even her date of birth is open to debate. However, we do know that it was in 1852, when Caroline was in her early or mid-twenties, that a twenty-four-year-old Swiss painter was introduced to the family. The initial relationship between Nicholas Chevalier and the Wilkie family was largely a professional one – Frederick took a fatherly interest in the younger artist, encouraged him in his painting and persuaded him to enter two watercolours in the Royal Academy Exhibition of 1852.

Exotic, ever charming, and dashingly handsome, Nicholas Chevalier must have swept the lovely Caroline off her feet. Certainly any English suitors would have paled into insignificance next to such a fine figure of romance. Born in St Petersburg, Nicholas was the son of a Russian mother and Swiss father. His father, Louis Chevalier, was in the employ of Prince de Wittgenstein, aide-de-camp to Czar Nicholas I, and it was on this prince's estate that Nicholas spent the first seventeen years of his life.

Then, in 1845, the family returned to Lausanne in Switzerland. Here Louis dissuaded Nicholas from the uncertainties of an artist's life and persuaded him to train as an architect. Over the following decade Nicholas studied art, architecture and painting in Lausanne and Munich before moving to London in about 1851. While in London he worked as a lithographer for Gruner, a designer who was preparing illustrations for publications such as *The Discoveries in the Ruins of Nineveh and Babylon.*

Not only did Chevalier further his painting career in London, he is said to have also designed the setting of the famous Koh-i-noor diamond for Queen Victoria. Another project involved the preparation of plans for a fountain in the grounds of the royal residence at Osborne. All the while we can suppose that his relationship with the Wilkie family in general, and Caroline in particular, quietly developed.

True love or not, the course of the relationship didn't quite run smooth. In 1853 and 1854, Nicholas's father sent him to study in Rome – a wonderful opportunity for Nicholas to develop his skill as a watercolourist, but not quite so handy for furthering his suit with Caroline. Nicholas may have initially intended to stay in Europe but his father became anxious about some investments he had made in Australia, and Nicholas's presence was required to help set the finances straight. He and his brother Thomas (later a prominent Melbourne photographer) arrived in Melbourne on Christmas Day 1854 and joined their elder brother Louis on his return from the Bendigo goldfields.

Their father's investments were found to have failed, and little could be done to retrieve the capital. Consequently, in early 1855 Nicholas was preparing to return to Europe (and Caroline). These plans were put in disarray when he received a very attractive offer – to be the cartoonist of the newly established *Melbourne Punch*. This was too good an opportunity for any aspiring young artist to turn down.

We have no diaries, love letters or contemporary comment to tell us of life and love in the Wilkie household, how love blossomed, or exactly at what point the lovers decided to wed. Absence certainly appears to have played some significant part in making the heart grow fonder as Caroline eventually sailed to Melbourne where she and Nicholas were married on 5 March 1857. There is a fine self-portrait of Nicholas painted as a present for his bride – it is tempting to think that he gave this to Caroline before he set sail for Australia, a very personal aide-mémoire for her sitting-room wall. Unfortunately no comparable portrait of Caroline is known to exist.

Melbourne-based illustrator, Edward La Trobe Bateman, later immortalised his dear friends' romance in verse, his tale implying that the engagement was a long-arranged 'understanding', vows lovingly exchanged before Nicholas set sail for southern lands:

> Nicholas C was a foreigner born
> With a crown often cropped, but a chin never shorn
> And like a true national Artist, would scorn
> To be anyone else but a foreigner born.

So Nicholas C got a pain in his side
Which all of the Kensington Doctors defied
And nothing could cure but at once to decide
To make Caroline W into his bride.

Caroline W sat at her tea
Sighing and thinking of Nicholas C
When a knock and a ring and a 'Who can it be?'
And standing and bowing before her was he.

Caroline W – do be my wife
And let us be one for the rest of our life.
And I swear we will never have trouble or strife
Till Time shall divide us in two with his knife.

Caroline W looked down her nose
Fiddled her fingers and twiddled her toes
And thought to herself as she heard him propose
She'd certainly faint in her tea-drinking clothes.

But Caroline W managed to stand
Managed to smile at the pleasure he planned
Managed to say in a voice very bland
'That he'd managed her heart, so might manage her hand'.

Bateman fancifully sets the wedding in Kensington rather than Melbourne, so may not be the most reliable narrator of events. However, 'Nichol' and 'Cary' were definitely devoted – certainly enough to move Edward Bateman to verse some years after their wedding. After five years of marriage nothing much seems to have changed:

Five years have floated adown the world's tide
Since Nichol and Cary were bridegroom and bride
Yet tho' tyrant Time their affection has tried
They still are like lovers by each other's side.

And once every year to the forest they stray
With provisions enough to refresh by the way
And there like two children at marriage they play
And live o'er again their first sweet wedding day.

Caroline would not have been without support in this new country as the Wilkie family had relations in Melbourne, including one Joseph Wilkie, owner of Wilkie's Pianoforte Saloon in Collins Street. Wilkie was a strong supporter of the arts and displayed the work of many prominent Melbourne artists in his front window – Nicholas's paintings were frequently hung here.

The Chevaliers were a popular Melbourne couple, their artistic and musical talents and general charm ensuring that they easily made friends with others of their background and interests. Nicholas was also greatly in demand as a painter, illustrator and designer. His talent as a landscape artist was quickly recognised, especially after he won a prize in a competition for the best picture by an artist in Australia. However, his was not a role that could be easily undertaken in comfortable residence at his Melbourne home. A colonial landscape artist's life was, of necessity, a travelling one.

Nicholas Chevalier came to New Zealand on 22 November 1865, full of resolve to visit 'the Switzerland of the Southern Hemisphere'. Here his work and reputation impressed the Dunedin public to such an extent that the Otago Provincial Council gave him a grant of £200 towards the expenses of making a pictorial survey of the region. It was hoped that this could be used to encourage immigration into the area.

The commission was excellent, but the life was lonely, involving travelling through the inland wilds of the southern lakes for four months. Caroline reports:

My husband had spent many months exploring and sketching the beauties of New Zealand, and had left me at our house in Melbourne, when finding many many months must still be occupied in his arduous though most interesting task; he therefore sent for me to join him, at least I was to stay with kind friends who invited me to make their house my home, until Mr Chevalier should have finished his sketching in Otago …

A wonderful idea in theory, but greatly complicated by the huge difficulties in communications with anyone in these early days of the colony. Caroline found the realities distinctly daunting.

> On my arrival at Dunedin … there was no good husband to meet me, and indeed no one, for no one knew I was coming and worse than all, no one … had … the slightest idea where he was. They only knew he had left some months before with three horses and his companion, with the intention of pushing as far up the province of Otago as possible and to stay as long as the provisions carried on his pack horse would last out. There was no letter from him, how could there be … My heart failed me …

A sleepless night ensued while Caroline deliberated as to what best to do. Waiting all alone in Dunedin for an indefinite length of time seemed a dreary option, so in the morning she re-boarded the steamer. Once at Port Lyttelton she set off to Christchurch to look up old friends from Melbourne, engineering contractor George Holmes and his wife. Disappointment ruled again as they were not at their Christchurch home. Undeterred, Caroline stayed the night before riding back to Lyttelton and taking a 'cockle shell' of a small steamer to their property at Pigeon Bay.

It must have been a massive relief to finally find a welcome in this strange country. 'Here my kind friends Mr and Mrs George Holmes welcomed me and … there I waited for seven long weeks, news of my husband. Sometimes I despaired, all sorts of fears came upon me …'

Nicholas eventually did arrive, over four months after he had left Melbourne, and almost two since Caroline had expected to meet with him in Dunedin. Travel weary after his 'tour through Otago and her grand lakes' he probably longed for a rest. Instead he returned to find that the Canterbury Provincial Council had followed Otago's example and were offering him £200 to complete a similar project. It was hardly a commission Nicholas could turn down and he lost no time in making arrangements for a trip through Canterbury (which at that stage included the West Coast) – at least this time he would have the company of Caroline.

Friends demurred, acquaintances shook their heads, but the Chevaliers were determined that Caroline should make the journey with Nicholas. Such an adventure, whatever the hardship, was irresistibly better than the prospect of waiting patiently in someone else's home.

This was to be no luxurious tour with an entourage of servants to carry Caroline's fine dresses and the makings of grand dinners. Accompanied by a hired man, Scott, and four newly acquired horses, they were to venture on a serious painting trip in some of the toughest country New Zealand had to offer. In a manner entirely alien to most genteel Victorian ladies, only the bare necessities were to be allowed. Caroline was given firm guidelines as to what she could pack.

> I was restricted to a small American cloth flat bag that would strap on my saddle, and fastened to the girth. It was no more than 12 inches by 12 inches and into that I had to put my wardrobe. How I did it I never can tell or what I carried but I had a change of linen and a thin silk dress that being light to carry, a pair of slippers for I had often wet feet, nay soaked feet. I had a good strong but short habit, and good riding trousers and shady hat. It is absolutely wonderful how little one does require, and how much one can dispense with.

Apart from this Caroline was allowed to carry practically nothing except another 'little American cloth bag with my sketch book over my shoulder'.

> There was very much to be done in buying stores, tea, sugar, flour, rice, hard dried meat they call junk [jerky], and a little butter (that did not last long). No milk, tinned milk was not then invented I think but no doubt we had some luxuries in the way of cheese or something portable.

The first night they slept in their tent – Caroline's first experience of camping out. She was less than enthusiastic:

> We had our supper, my first camp one. The tin panikin with the hot tea burnt my lips, and with no milk, was not very nice, but we had bread brought with us and really delicious, [with] some butter or cheese … As it was quite dry, we lay on the earth … Nicholas thought nothing of the hard ground, I thought it hard. Our pillows were our saddles and I remember always how terribly mine smelt …

'**Wet or fine?**' *Attributed to Nicholas Chevalier but probably by Caroline.* 1866.
A-102-034, ALEXANDER TURNBULL LIBRARY, WELLINGTON.

On subsequent nights Caroline slept rather better:

[We] made luxurious beds of cut fern, sweet and soft … Sleeping in a tent is an extraordinary sensation. You seem to be in the open air, and the thin kind of calico appears lighter somehow than when out in the open. You wake up and it all seems white and dazzling, but certainly one sleeps well in that pure air and I never once suffered from insomnia. Not as one often does in a luxurious bed and beautiful room.

Camp cookery, necessary for producing the daily damper, was a challenging and time-consuming process. The oven had to be built, 'a large fire made … until there was a large heap of red hot ashes, broad and high enough for the oven'. The centre was scooped out and the damper placed inside.

This said loaf was very large quite eight inches across and took a long time, but when finished was really very nice indeed … It was all right that night for supper, but the next day – I could not bite it, it was hard as possible but the others thought it perfection, and I had to make up my mind

'A boggy pass.' *Attributed to Nicholas Chevalier but probably by Caroline. 1866.*
A-102-030, ALEXANDER TURNBULL LIBRARY, WELLINGTON.

to eat it somehow, or go without.

The path to the headwaters of the Hurunui was especially narrow and precip-
itous, with a rapid torrent far below and a wall of boulders rising on the other
side. Caroline had one of the most terrifying moments of the whole journey
when her saddle slipped around and she came off her horse. Poor Nicholas
was perhaps even more frightened a few minutes later when he saw Caroline's
riderless horse come over the hill. It was a vast relief to reach the head of
the Hurunui and cross over to the other side of the alpine divide to 'where the
fine river Teramakau [sic] rises'.

Their next challenge was an area where the mud was terrible, made even
more unpleasant by a tangle of underlying roots – this made the terrain
so treacherous that it was impossible to ride with any degree of safety. Caroline
hated this, but stalwartly did her best to improvise suitable attire:

We were all far above our ankles in mud, and once or twice nearly up
to the knees. I had luckily two pieces of American cloth to keep the wet
off my sketch book and these I bound round my legs like putties, and so

really did not get very wet, but my boots well I thought they would never reach Hokitika; but they did.

Things looked a little better as evening came on and the party had to make their first crossing of the Taramakau.

> It looked nothing at all to do and most picturesque, but it was far from agreeable [with] huge moving boulders and all more or less slimy, so that one had to be on the look out, and make a dash at a given moment ... I was intently watching and just starting, when the wretched lawyer, a hanging plant with long reversed hook or thorns all down its long spray caught my hat and my hair and nearly made me a second Absolom.

It was probably fortunate that space restrictions had prevented Caroline from packing a mirror. She relied on the fabled 'Narcissus mirror' for most of the journey, noting that: 'Once awake one is only too glad to rise, and then one has to find a little creek or bend in the river or lake, and make one's ablution, and a still pool for a looking glass.'

One camp, close to the headwaters of the Taramakau, was particularly fine, with clean water to wash out their clothes and a roaring fire to dry them by. However, Caroline was distinctly doleful about her attire because, although her improvised gaiters proved most successful at keeping out both water and mud, her riding dress was a different matter. 'My habit was in a miserable plight and I looked at it in dismay, for I thought it would not possibly be dry for the morning. Dry or not it had to be put on.'

That apart, the camp was idyllic, a fine resting place after crossing the alpine divide.

> We had a most comfortable supper and again I cut the bracken and our beds were soft. The aromatic pillow, I had become accustomed to, and slept most soundly. The music of the river was our lullaby, and the singing or chirping of the birds our morning song. My husband sketched till he could no longer see, and Scott nodded beside the blazing fire. How grand the range looked over which we had crossed, wild and beautiful, but I had no desire to make that experience again. Riding was bad enough, walking

worse but struggling through up nearly to one's knees in mud worsest.

The next day brought fine fare, offered generously by two drovers.

> Rough men, and poor hard workers. They looked at me with the greatest astonishment. They rose at once, and helped me dismount, gave to me the best seat (a stone) near the fire, and then went to assist the artist and his man ... and aiding us to get our mid day meal of damper [and] cheese ... But what did I see a frying pan and in that frying pan, some mutton. I had no sooner exclaimed the word than frying pan, mutton and all were handed to me ... The generous lordly way in which it was done, was better than any banquet of costly viands ... The cooking was not that of a chef, but a good appetite is better with the roughest fare than dainty dishes and indigestion.

Once closer to the coast other accommodation options became available, but these could certainly be 'much worse than camping'. At one small accommodation house they were not only overcharged by the proprietor, but also distinctly unnerved by the company.

> There were a set of horrible fellows, squatting about drinking and smoking, and they would think nothing of taking horses or anything they could lay their hands on ... You can imagine that the faces of these kind of men gave you fear.

This was no undue anxiety – the Chevaliers had very good cause for concern during these rough days of West Coast gold. It was only a few months later that George Dobson, assistant provincial engineer and surveyor at Hokitika, and brother of Nicholas's friend Arthur Dobson, was robbed and murdered by a gang who mistook him for a storekeeper carrying gold dust.

The Chevaliers were given an earthen-floored room to sleep in, rubbish and piles of wood around, their beds little more than wooden 'shelves' on the wall. Fortunately they had their own blankets as the ones they were given were so dirty as to be unusable. However, the matter of bedding proved to be the least of their worries that night. When Caroline looked through the inch-wide

'**Tomboy very wild.**' *Attributed to Nicholas Chevalier but probably by Caroline. 1866.*
A-102-032, ALEXANDER TURNBULL LIBRARY, WELLINGTON.

chinks in the wall beside her berth she saw the men in fearsome mood:

> ... many half drunk, all noisy, some miserable, some wild . . . They were
> drinking beer ... and smoking ... Their conversation was not agreeable,
> some were most quarrelsome, and we unfortunate people seemed the
> theme of a deal of unpleasantness. We were talked of indirectly as con-
> founded aristocrats, and upstarts and every name they could think of
> because I had not gone in and sat down with them.

Nicholas and Caroline felt huge relief when the proprietor turned all the men
out at 10 o'clock and rode away. It seemed that at last they would be able to
sleep in peace. But it was not to be so straightforward.

> Alas, alas – in less than ten minutes the place was alive ... with rats ...
> that rushed up and down on the table, over the chairs, along the rafters,
> all around the fire and packed along close to the chinks, squeaking and
> running. This was too dreadful ... nothing could be done but get a candle
> and sit up till morning ... It was one of the most dreadful nights I have
> passed ... I never shall forget those horrid creatures sitting on the tables
> on their hind legs and eating every scrap and crumb they could find and
> fighting with each other.

The next challenge was the aptly named Taipo ('little devil') river – small, but very rapid and dangerous.

> Surely it was a demon in truth. It was not only a rushing mass of water but the whole was a mass of high boulders. There seemed not a place for a horse to put its foot. I well remember, that I felt quite un-nerved, and almost hoped that my husband would consider I could not pass it. Far from that, he simply treated it as a thing that must be done, and I had to do it …

Matters weren't made any easier by the nervous disposition of Caroline's horse.

> My horse Tomboy, had little courage, was soon tired and unfortunately had a sore shoulder, from an ill fitting saddle. I had great difficulty to make him follow and he knew full well I was funky myself …

> … Indeed there was nothing to be done but rush it, and I really did. The absolute crossing I cannot remember although I had tucked my skirt high up, I was wet through, what with the splash and the deep waters. All I thought of was my poor brute's fetlocks and should we get to the other side … it was an awful scramble and [I] thanked God when at last we all stood on the other side, and found the horses were all right, but the trembling of my poor beast was quite painful to see.

They had another major river crossing the following day – the Taramakau, now greatly changed to a wide open river, at times so deep that the horses had to swim. Caroline and the packhorse's load ('all our impedimenta') were paddled across in a 'tubby boat' while the men rode their horses, and led the others. They then repacked and started off once more.

Pitching the tent for evening camp was always a challenge – it wasn't just important to find a dry flat spot for the tent, it was essential that there should be good grass for the horses as well. Exhausted after their river crossings and wet from rain, Caroline was only too pleased when they pitched tent by the river that night. 'I began to unpack and prepare our evening meal, getting each day a more frugal one.'

This evening Nicholas became increasingly uneasy about the steadily falling rain, and with good cause. Half an hour after they had set up camp the river had risen so considerably that Nicholas insisted that everything must be repacked and a safer camp found. This was trying for them all, but especially miserable for Caroline.

> When the tent was taken down and folded it was so heavy from the rain that it was as much as N. and Scott could lift it on the pack horse, who simply groaned at its weight. As for myself, I was cross and miserable and I expect it nearly wanted two to lift me into the saddle so stiff and tired I was. But there was no help for it and though darkness had set in we must trudge for safe quarters.

They set off in search of a surveyor's house they had heard of, no easy venture.

> It seemed interminable, and one or two hour's travelling slowly, without light and very tired, appeared endless, so much so that I begged we might camp. But there was no grass for the horses and no water for ourselves, and N. was determined to go on and on.

Eventually the party arrived at 'a real house, a corrugated iron house with doors and windows and at the sides [a] long corrugated stable for a number of horses'. The bedraggled party of strangers were all immediately '... made "at home" and never was a house before so like a palace to me. Wet and tired, and hungry. There was a large open fire place, with big logs burning, and seats and a nice table, yes even a table cloth, for supper was just about to begin.' The two surveyors and their man generously shared their meal, a veritable feast of damper, meat and cheese topped off with a most delicious steaming hot plum pudding.

Nicholas and Caroline were now given the surveyors' stretchers – luxury indeed to lie in comfort while the storm burst and the rain poured in deafening torrents on their corrugated iron shelter. 'The gratitude and thankfulness we both felt to be under that frail roof did not require words. Had we been on the river, our little camp must have been swept away and the horses ... would have been carried down the river and we should never have been heard of [again].'

These surveyors were entirely different from other men they had encountered en route. One of them '... was a most gentlemanly and charming man, and one wondered how he could be in such an out of the way part of the world. His only companion, Mr Aitken, also a very nice young engineer.'

Mr Aitken offered to ride with them as far as Hokitika, an offer gladly accepted by the travel-worn trio. They reached the coast after dark and rode along the beach in a thunderstorm, an unnerving experience for both riders and horses.

It was pitch dark save for the flashes of lightening which illumined all around. The rain came down in torrents and we were all wet through. It was a moment of horror for me, and when we came to a stream that flows down to the sea, which rushed down, and the waves with high foam rushed up and raised the water very high, my horse would not face it, turned, jibbed, and I having no courage could not make him take it ...

... I determined rather to ford it myself and slipt right off my saddle, when Mr Aitken dropt off his [and] caught me round the waist and seizing the reins of my horse carried me across just between the surging and rising waves. It was a horrible moment, and I thought it must be the last for our party.

Soaked to the skin and hungry, with Caroline tired to breaking point, the party pushed doggedly on to Hokitika where they asked for a bed at the best of the rough drinking and sleeping places frequented by the gold diggers. They were clearly unwelcome: the proprietor was 'a queer looking individual who eyed me up and down, and then informed me that his house was full and he had no place for a woman. This was very evident.'

A much smarter house, complete with flagstaff, door and windows brought more joy to the bedraggled party. Here Nicholas recognised the proprietor as a former waiter at his favourite Melbourne restaurant and spoke to him in German. Suddenly they were made most welcome, a fire was lit, a room provided and Caroline was only too happy 'to change my soaking clothes for the one change I carried in my little wallet'. It was a highlight to go downstairs to share an excellent supper with the odd assortment of men who lived in the house.

Hokitika was very much a frontier gold town, 'a very wild place and queer dreadful men were about. Desperate characters they looked.' Caroline noted 90 public houses in this rough little settlement. She also walked up and down the banks of the Kanieri [Kaniere] River and watched the gold diggers working along its banks. Two shipwrecks on the river bar gave an aura of misery and, all in all, Caroline considered Hokitika a 'God Forsaken place'.

There were just a few respectable citizens including the commissioner and magistrate responsible for keeping order and allotting the mining operations and diggings. The two or three ladies in the town quickly called on Caroline, giving her the warmest of welcomes. Not only were they very kind to Caroline but they were in great awe of the journey she had made – all of them had arrived rather more sedately by steamer.

This little bit of 'society' presented Caroline with a challenge – how to be smart enough? 'I had by the one little thin silk dress and with this I had to be very smart. When the habit was dry I wore that …'

A highlight of the Chevaliers' Hokitika stay was a picnic, especially arranged so that Caroline could see the ferns up the Kaniere River. The ferns were beautiful but, in true West Coast style, 'the weather turned to pouring rain and by the time we reached our place for the picnic we were very wet. We all made the best of it and enjoyed every thing in spite of the many disagreeables.' Despite the rain, the picnic was done in some style. A sketch by Nicholas depicts the scene – a long table set elegantly under the trees, the lake behind with the boat tied to a tree, the party standing or seated around. Chairs don't seem to feature and the weather appears fine – presumably once the rain came Nicholas's sketch book would have disappeared as fast as the picnic!

While Nicholas travelled on to Greymouth to paint, Caroline stayed with her new-found friends, all delighted to have such a charming companion for a week or so. Then it was back over the Alps to Christchurch, past dramatic mountain scenery, wonderful trees and ferns. Travelling continued to be challenging, but accommodation houses were cheerful, the weather generally good and Nicholas sketched at every opportunity – all seemed relatively civilised after the rigours of crossing the Hurunui Saddle and unbridged rivers. They had an especially delightful diversion when asked to stay at Ben More station one night, a spot notable for its charming buildings and merry company.

'Picnic given by Dr Ryley of the Hokitika Hospital.' *Nicholas Chevalier, 1866.*
B.038958, MUSEUM OF NEW ZEALAND TE PAPA TONGAREWA, WELLINGTON.

Throughout the journey the not-so-wild native birds enchanted Caroline and Nicholas alike.

> At this camp the inquisitive little bird, the weka, came at once, prying in and out, looking so cleverly at everything, pulling it, and pecking what it could eat. It was so pretty to watch it … Then the wild birds did not fear man … and came around you and when you sketched hopped even on the book. One day a robin jumped on to the large drawing board Nicholas had on his lap and looked at his work, I hope approvingly.

This is a rare reference to Caroline sketching on this journey. However, if her sketchbook hadn't been important to her she would never have included it in her limited kit – we can suppose that she often sat companionably drawing by Nicholas's side as he worked on his ever increasing collection of sketches. If she could muster the energy that is – it was an exhausting journey for the diminutive Caroline who, in contrast to Nicholas, is unlikely to have been particularly physically fit before they set off.

'Riding alone for days … is most trying but when one adds sketching, continually taking notes and now and then getting out your colours. The day itself is far too short, but fatigue comes and night is then a blessing.' Caroline omits to mention the other camp duties: cutting bracken for their beds, collecting wood and cooking damper, preparing some culinary delights out of dried meat and rice, washing and drying her hopelessly impractical clothes. It is not so much her lack of sketches that is surprising, but rather that she had time or enthusiasm for any art at all.

Although there are no known drawings by Caroline, some of the more humorous sketches previously attributed to Nicholas may well be hers. The style of these is distinctly different from most of Nicholas's works, images boldly drawn with a strong sense of the ridiculous.

The Chevaliers eventually returned to Christchurch on 16 May 1866, some seven weeks after their departure from Pigeon Bay. Nicholas gave himself very little time for rest – he had now to paint other areas of Canterbury in order to complete his commission for the Canterbury Provincial Government. Dated sketches indicate that he was on the road again by 29 May, this time travelling without Caroline. This sketching tour lasted till the end of June and it is believed that once again Caroline stayed with friends, probably with Mr and Mrs Holmes as well as with Mrs von Haast, wife of Nicholas's friend Julius von Haast.

July was the time of reckoning as far as the public was concerned. They certainly weren't disappointed – exhibitions in Christchurch, Wellington and Dunedin included more than two hundred works. Equally impressive was the fact that in eight months Nicholas had journeyed over 3500 miles and visited nineteen lakes from Lake Manapouri to Lake Brunner. It was a remarkable achievement.

Back in Melbourne Nicholas took up a position with *The Australian Illustrated News*, a position that was to closely involve him with the visit of the Duke of Edinburgh, second son of Queen Victoria. As the representative for his paper Nicholas travelled with the Duke's party as it toured through Victoria, greatly impressing the prince not only with his skill as a painter, a musician and a linguist but also with his extremely agreeable manner. A close relationship developed between the prince and the painter and when the duke visited Tasmania, Nicholas was included in the royal party.

Nicholas and Caroline returned to New Zealand in November 1868, spending two months painting in the North Island – a fascinating visit during a period of land wars. Nicholas found Wanganui under siege and recorded much of what he saw in a series of sketches.

While in New Zealand Nicholas received an invitation to join the royal party on the last leg of its world tour and therefore the Chevaliers returned to Sydney, somewhat prematurely, at the end of December. Here they joined the Duke of Edinburgh on the HMS *Galatea*. Nicholas was now an essential part of the duke's entourage. Although it is never clearly stated, Caroline is sure to have been on board as well. She later mentions a diary of the tour, but unfortunately this has not survived.

This journey gave Nicholas more opportunities to add to his already large collection of New Zealand paintings, as the royal party sailed to New Zealand for an official visit of about six weeks' duration before heading 'Home'.

It was a long return journey for Nicholas and Caroline. The flotilla (with the Chevaliers probably both accompanying the duke's immediate party on the *Galatea*) finally left Auckland on 27 May. From here the royal party sailed to Tahiti, Hawaii, Japan, China and Singapore in 1869 and then on to Calcutta and Ceylon in 1870. The voyage must have been any artist's dream – to accompany a royal patron on a grand journey around the world.

And it certainly was grand – beautiful paintings completed by Nicholas on the *Galatea* show the royal party gathered on the occasion of a concert. The setting is so splendid that one presumes that the ship was in port, the occasion orchestrated to impress some foreign potentate. A fountain is shown bravely playing inside a 'concert hall' and opulent crystal chandeliers hang from the ceiling. Potted palms, flags and banners complete the decoration.

There are two paintings, quite complementary. One looks past the fountain and potted palms to the stage where the show in progress. The other is from the other direction – the fountain, palms and flags are once more in evidence, with neatly turned-out sailors sitting to one side while elegant ladies of the court adorn the other. Caroline is likely to have been one of the company here, sitting with the other ladies (royal and aspiring to be!) enjoying the ship's entertainment.

There is no doubt that travelling with the prince would have been very different from Caroline's previous experiences of the rigours of shipboard life. This time the food would have been prepared by one of the royal chefs, the cabins, dining and sitting areas she used luxurious rather than utilitarian. It wasn't just a matter of keeping the royal party in comfort and elegance – such a flotilla was literally 'flying the flag' for Empire, showcasing not just royal, but British Imperial style. They are sure to have had the best that practicality could allow – this was high living on the ocean waves.

Back in Britain, Nicholas's star remained high in the royal firmament. The Chevaliers settled in some style in Hyde Park in London, an address befitting someone with strong royal patronage. From the time of their return in 1870 until early 1888 Nicholas was engaged by the Royal Court to record important events in Queen Victoria's reign.

Nicholas was busy in many other areas as well. In 1872 he held an extensive exhibition at the Crystal Palace and he also exhibited from time to time in the Royal Academy and the Salon. His well-known work 'The Opening of the International Exhibition, Vienna, 1873', which was shown at the Royal Academy in 1877, received glowing reviews. It is likely that this was painted on a trip that Caroline refers to at the end of her New Zealand diary. She notes that Nicholas (and herself perhaps as well) was 'Taken by the Prince of Wales to Vienna, staid [sic] at Palace in Brussels, in Palace in Vienna and Darmstaat. Received by Empress. Saw Princess Alice.'

The most notable occasion was doubtless the marriage of Nicholas's old friend the Duke of Edinburgh in St Petersburg in 1874. It is to be hoped that Caroline travelled with Nicholas, enjoying the drama and opulence of this royal match.

We know little about what Caroline did to pass her days – she may have painted but no work survives to tell the tale. However, we can presume that, along with Nicholas, she would have been active in spheres other than painting. A devoted wife, in later years she wrote notes on Nicholas's life to aid any future biographer, all the while leaving little or no mention of herself. Caroline was frustratingly self-effacing.

Always a keen musician, Nicholas was a founder member of the Royal Orchestral Society. He also always maintained contact with New Zealand, keeping in touch with his friend Sir Julius von Haast. In 1872 he sought the assistance of the South Kensington Museum in obtaining material for the Christchurch Museum.

Nicholas's health deteriorated from 1885, prompting the Chevaliers to spend their winters in much milder Madeira, where Nicholas explored and painted. He stopped painting in 1893 and retired with Caroline to a 'Swiss chalet' he had built in London. Nicholas died of a cerebral haemorrhage on 15 March 1902 at the Chevaliers' London house.

Caroline was in her mid-sixties at the time of Nicholas's death and was to live another fifteen years. It was during this time that she set pen to paper and wrote her 'Short Description of a Journey across the Southern Island of New Zealand ...' Completed in 1908 this constitutes a significant contribution to early travel writing in New Zealand. Caroline is reputed to be the first European woman to complete this gruelling transalpine journey.

Caroline's other major contribution is the role she played in furthering the reputation of Nicholas. Ever the devoted artist's wife, she appears to have consistently supported him with little or no thought to her own career. In 1907, after Nicholas's death, she presented many of his New Zealand works to the National Art Gallery in Wellington. Four more paintings were received from her estate in 1918.

Aged in her early eighties, Caroline died in a nursing home in Bournemouth on 26 December 1917.

BIBLIOGRAPHY

Bateman, Edward La Trobe. 'Scratches and Sketches by a Wandering Artist, 1854–1885.' MS BAT, Alexander Turnbull Library, Wellington.

Chevalier, Caroline. 'A Short Description of a Journey across the Southern Island of New Zealand from East Coast to West Coast and back from West Coast to East Coast.' (1908 typescript). QMS-0438, Alexander Turnbull Library, Wellington.

Day, Melvin N. *Nicholas Chevalier: His Life and Work with Special Reference to his Career* *In New Zealand and Australia.* Wellington: Millwood, 1981.

Porter, Frances and MacDonald, Charlotte (Eds). *My Hand Will Write What My Heart Dictates.* Auckland: Auckland University Press, Bridget Williams Books, 1996.

Roberts, Neil. *Nicholas Chevalier, An Artist's Journey Through Canterbury in 1866.* Christchurch: Robert McDougall Art Gallery, 1992.

The Dictionary of New Zealand Biography. Vol 1. Wellington: Bridget Williams Books, Department of Internal Affairs.

MARY DOBIE
1850 – 1880

DREADFUL MURDER AT OPUNAKE. A YOUNG LADY KILLED. HER HEAD NEARLY SEVERED FROM HER BODY. MAN ARRESTED ON SUSPICION OF THE MURDER.[1]

… The particulars … are that Miss Dobie, a sister-in-law of Major Goring, of the A.C. Force [Armed Constabulary], went for a walk yesterday afternoon, and as she did not return by dusk, a search party was sent out to look for her, when her body was found … amongst the flax, with her clothes in great disorder, and with her throat cut – her head being nearly severed from her body.

The body was finally found with the help of Miss (Mary) Dobie's faithful dogs, 'her great pets and almost constant companions'. Elsewhere it was variously reported that an old saddle, a piece of bridle, some bloodstained trousers and 'a bunch of flowers, evidently gathered by the deceased' were found near a trail of blood among the flax bushes. Traces of a desperate struggle were evident.

    The unfortunate Mary Beatrix Dobie was an English lady, a keen traveller

[1] Excerpt from the *Taranaki Herald*, 26 November 1880.

'Tea party in our cabin.' *Mary Dobie, 1877.*

REPRODUCED BY COURTESY OF MARGARET DRAKE BROCKMAN.

and a talented artist. Born in 1850, she was one of the six children of Herbert Main Dobie, a major in the East India Army, and Ellen Locker, daughter of a prominent Cumbrian family. Mary's uncle was Frederick Locker, editor and owner of the London-based newspaper, *The Graphic*, a paper to which Mary frequently contributed illustrations.

On 1 October 1877, at the age of twenty-seven, Mary set sail for New Zealand with her mother and her sister Bertha to join Mary's brother Herbert, an engineer engaged in building railways in the fledgling colony. From the day they embarked on the three-masted, full-rigged ship, the *May Queen*, the two sisters kept a record of their travels. However, although the diary of the voyage is meant to be a combined effort, Mary's written contributions are somewhat meagre.

Mary may have written little, but her sketches and watercolours colourfully complement Bertha's text, quietly bringing this shipboard journey to life. Mary depicts passengers and crew in moments of work and leisure – we see the saloon (first-class) passengers eating at the Captain's table, a refined tea party

LADY TRAVELLERS

'Saloon passengers sitting down for dinner.' *Mary Dobie, 1877.*
REPRODUCED BY COURTESY OF MARGARET DRAKE BROCKMAN.

in the Dobies' cabin, the ladies exercising on deck and Bertha knitting. The Captain is captured reading a nautical sermon at Sunday service, while sailors are shown stitching sails and supervising Mary and Bertha as they haul in the log line. Some men are sketched singing, others reading, another having his hair cut. The ship's Christmas tree is drawn, along with Captain Tatchell in his Father Christmas get-up. And it's not just people that Mary portrays so well: she also paints the *May Queen* in fair weather and foul, swept by the sea and sailing south in the cold company of icebergs.

There was certainly plenty of time for artists and diarists. The *May Queen* took ninety-nine days to sail through temperate, tropical and sub-antarctic waters en route to landfall at Auckland. At times they were becalmed, but generally the ship made excellent progress, racing across the ocean at speeds of thirteen knots or more – on one day she covered a remarkable 320 miles in twenty-four hours!

Luckily the Dobies were all excellent sailors, their appetite never impaired by even the worst of weather:

Sunday, October 6th. Weather warmer each day. Getting on rapidly. Not so many to breakfast – fellow passengers feeling very ill. We sympathised fully with them and I'm afraid they hated us for being so horrid and well.

They may have been well, but the Dobie ladies still suffered unusual challenges from the ship's movement.

1st Sunday at sea. Smartened ourselves … Difficulties at breakfast, ship rolling – great delight by all when Bertha's cup of tea went up her sleeve … In fear of a sea bursting over us … The Sermon disappointing … some preferred watching the splendid coamers coming over the bulwarks.

Bertha carefully records everyday details of shipboard life. After the first week at sea she notes:

Wind still fair and we are doing about 9 knots steadily.
… got up at 7.30.
Breakfast 9.0 o'clock. Had for breakfast currie and rice.
Dinner 2.0 Beef steak, dry mashed potatoes.
Tea 6.0 Irish stew, sometimes as a treat.
Bed 10.0 Toast, tea and coffee.
On Sundays for dinner, either pea soup or broth, roast beef, boiled mutton, plum duff, roast ducks, chickens, pork and haricot – damson pie, gooseberry pie, jam tart, rice and currants.

The cook rather too fond of onions, cheese old and new, water …

Lat. 37.26 Long. 16.29 230 miles since noon yesterday.

Wednesday, October 10th
Just a week since we left Gravesend … it seems to fly, one has so much to do, working, reading, tidying our cabin, singing, playing games, tramping the deck etc. etc.

… No-one has mentioned our hours for meals etc., so I will now give a description of our day. We are called at 7.30 when we go in turn to the bathroom and have a delicious salt water bath, Bertha always the first, go on deck at 8.0, have time for a quiet little read, then knit, nibble biscuits etc, till 9.0 when we have breakfast. Spend the morning in writing, making our cabin neat, working and reading. Dinner at 2.0. Afternoon much the same as morning. Tea at 6.0, evening chiefly spent playing games etc. To bed about 10.0. It is certainly a very pleasant life and I enjoy it thoroughly, but all the same I want to be in England now-w-w.

Entertainment was home-grown, frivolity largely dependent on the compatibility of the Dobies' ten fellow saloon passengers and, on occasion, selected second and third class travellers. Concerts were popular – the piano played a crucial role here. Invitations were sent out by the midday 'post' for tea parties and there was even an 'At Home' in the Dobies' cabin. And, when the mood took, dancing provided fitness and fun in the evening hours:

Friday, October 12th
Nothing particular happened until the evening, when we danced on the poop by moonlight, to a cornet played by a 2nd class passenger – Mr. Stuart and Mary danced the Demerara gallop which she must illustrate ... We are the only ladies who dance, except in a quadrille when Mother and Mrs Wilson joined.

During the day, passengers kept themselves busy by writing diaries and letters home and planning shipboard social activities. Reading, knitting and lace making were popular occupations. Bertha remarks: '... Finished a foot of point lace, have been three weeks at it, working steadily.' Games are frequently mentioned. Chess, Napoleon and Whist are played and Bertha gleefully writes: 'Had some singing and I spambled Mother at Bezique.'

A little later, in the tropics:

Thursday, October 18th
Very hot day, sort of damp steaming heat. We were made to read again after dinner, and kept at it till the tea bell rang. Played games of sorts in the evening, on deck: Lights, Buzz, Characters, 20 Questions, acting

adverbs and stool of repentance. Nearly everyone joined – such a hot night. Some of the gentlemen slept on deck. Becalmed for a time.

Then we are treated to a rare note from Mary, writing about herself in the third person:

> Mary has been very naughty, never writing any diary, but it's so hot and she is too limp. Thermo: 85 down below. Oh, the meals are fearful! She cannot eat. Dinner is the worst – she has given up soup now – and the whole of the meal. She is thinking how soon she can leave the table without people thinking she is sea sick ... The evening is the time we all look forward to ... Lovely moonlight evenings – sea soft and grey, a great quiet and calmness, then we sit, lean against the rail, lie on deck and give ourselves up to enjoyment and laziness. Listen to singing on the main deck by the 2nd and 3rd class passengers – sailors sing on the forecastle then we end by singing ourselves.

Physical exercise was diligently worked at – as much for warmth as for fitness once the *May Queen* got to the icy southern seas. The passengers played games in the saloon in order to get warm and other games were played with 'beanbags' on deck during the day. Walking proved ever popular, especially with Bertha who, weather permitting, walked the deck for long periods – generally at least three miles a day.

Once in the southern seas, the enervating heat of the tropics was only a fond memory, a far remove from the icebergs that now loomed large around the ship.

> Sunday, December 1st
> We slept late as we had not had a very good night, the ship rolling tremendously and going a great rate 14 knots a good part of the time, also there was no bath to be had ... about 11, heard a cry of ice-berg on the lee-bow and whizzed up to see it. So very lovely, about 14 miles off, like a rock of greenish crystal with the spray breaking right up to the top of it, from the force of the waves ... They say the ice-berg wd have reached higher than our mast-head.

Shipboard studies. *Mary Dobie, 1877.*

93

'Bertha and Mary hauling in the logline.' *Mary Dobie, 1877.*
REPRODUCED BY COURTESY OF MARGARET DRAKE BROCKMAN.

Thursday, December 6th
Mary and I [went] for a walk before dinner and tea in the rain which kept
on all day. We helped haul in the log-line which warmed us well, the second time we did it alone … Had a concert in the evening – quiet night.
A sailor had to hold the log line as we hauled for fear it should slip and
run away again. Concert in the evening. Averill gave me a lovely laniard
for my fan.

Monday, December 10th
… there was snow, so Mary and I went up and had great fun snowballing
… Busy practising both morning and afternoon for a scotch concert which
took place in the evening, nothing but scotch songs, reading etc.

The *May Queen* dropped anchor in Auckland Harbour at 5.30 a.m. on 7
January 1878, some fourteen weeks after the Dobies first boarded the ship at
Gravesend. Herbert was there to meet his family and quickly installed them in
'May Cottage … a very pretty little wooden house, one storied with verandahs
both at the front and the back'. He had been there for six weeks already, busy
making furniture for the rooms and preparing the garden. Even more exciting
was the prospect of meeting Herbert's fiancée, Charlotte or 'Tottie' Gilfillan.
Bertha later enthuses:

We are delighted with Tottie and when I say I am perfectly satisfied with her as a sister-in-law and wd not wish her changed in any way, I can't say more I think. She is very small with wee hands and feet, decidedly pretty and rosy and merry looking with dark brown curling hair. She is the eldest of seven, and was 18 last week. We like her mother and the children too.

Once in New Zealand the family's travels continued. In 1879 Mary, Bertha and Herbert went to Fiji where they stayed with the Governor, Sir Arthur Gordon. This trip appears to have been a great success. Sir Arthur was reported as having 'much admired the talent of the young lady' (Mary). Mary sketched at every opportunity and prepared a series of illustrated articles on Fiji. These were published in the *London Graphic* as 'A ride through the Northern district of the colony, illustrated by sketches'.

Back in Auckland, Mary involved herself in the local amateur theatre. In 1880 her performance as Lydia Languish in *The Rivals* was much admired. She and her mother then set off to tour the North Island prior to their return to England.

Although none of the Dobie women had ever intended to stay in New Zealand for more than a couple of years, Bertha's plans changed significantly after she met, and presumably fell in love with, Major Forster Yelverton Goring of the New Zealand Regiment. A veteran of the land wars, Major Goring was an extremely capable officer who had distinguished himself in a number of actions. His father was Forster Goring, Clerk of the New Zealand Executive Council, while his mother was of aristocratic birth: formerly the Hon Sydney Yelverton, she was the daughter of Viscount Avonmore of Bellisle, Tipperary, Ireland. This was an excellent match by any standards. Bertha married her major in 1880 and moved with him to Taranaki where he was the commanding officer of the Cape Egmont camp.

In November 1880 Mary and her mother were making their farewell trip to the Gorings. Despite simmering unrest over land issues in the Taranaki district, it does not appear that the visitors had previously felt at all under threat. Mary had already travelled extensively around the immediate district, painting at every opportunity, with no escort other than her little black dogs. On the day of her murder she had gone to sketch at 'one of the most beautiful spots in the district', Te Namu Bay, scene of the

New Zealand sketches. *Mary Dobie, 1877.*

1862 wreck of the ship *Lord Worsley*.

Events moved quickly once Mary's mutilated body was discovered. One man was arrested almost immediately – Walter Stannard, a horse-breaker, had the misfortune to appear on the scene with blood on his hat, clothes and boots. Three days later a twenty-year-old Maori man, Te Karea or Tuhi, was also arrested for the murder. The *Taranaki Herald* described Tuhi as 'not at all repulsive looking, on the contrary, his features have a mild and rather intelligent expression which makes it rather hard to believe him capable of an act of such unparalleled ferocity'.

At the inquest on 29 November, Walter Stannard was discharged due to lack of evidence against him – it had been found that the blood was from his horse's bleeding nose. The *Taranaki Herald* then continues: 'On the native prisoner Tuhi … being asked if he wished to make any statement he replied: "Yes; I did it, I am the murderer." … On being told that he was committed to take his trial at the next sitting of the Supreme Court at New Plymouth, he said "I do not wish for another trial; kill me at once; I am the murderer."'

When Tuhi was tried on 13 December he was inevitably found guilty and sentenced to death. Retribution was rapid in these colonial days. Tuhi was led to the gallows in Wellington gaol on Christmas Eve, 1880, almost exactly one month after Mary Dobie's brutal murder.

POSTSCRIPT

After her return to England Mrs Dobie settled in the small village of Irthington, near Carlisle.

In 1885 Major Goring was promoted to Colonel and appointed first Commanding Officer to the newly raised New Zealand Permanent Artillery. He was initially appointed Commander of the Dunedin district, but was subsequently transferred to Auckland. When he retired he became an orchardist. He and Bertha made at least two trips 'Home' to England – the editor of the Dobie diaries remembers Bertha visiting her grandmother (Bertha's niece) in the late 1920s.

BIBLIOGRAPHY

Dobie, Bertha and Mary. *The Voyage of the May Queen*. Ed Margaret Drake Brockman.

Braunton Devon: Merlin Books Ltd, 1992.

Dyne, D.G. *Famous N.Z. Murders*. Auckland and London: Fontana Silver Fern, 1974.

CONSTANCE ASTLEY
1851 – 1935

MARGARET'S LETTER MADE ME SO DESPERATELY ANXIOUS AND SAD BECAUSE SHE TELLS ME THAT YOU ARE NOT BEING NEARLY SO CAREFUL AS I BELIEVED AND HOPED YOUR LOVE FOR ALL OF US WOULD MAKE YOU – she says she feels like a spy to be telling me but as she had once written to me soon after you went Home setting my mind at rest to that habit of getting into bed with Connie … she thought she ought to tell me or I would be being cheated … I feel very angry with dear Connie for even wanting you to be so near to her … I long to have you out of reach of Connie … and my heart sank when I heard she was to follow you to Arles …

Alla, sister of the noted Wellington painter Dorothy (Dolla) Richmond, writes to Dolla on 26 November 1901 expressing the concern of family and friends about Dolla's relationship with Constance (Connie) Astley, English gentlewoman and traveller. While visiting New Zealand in 1897 and 1898, Connie had entered into a passionate affair with Dolla. The lovers parted when Connie returned to Scotland in April 1898 but were reunited the following

Constance Astley on a Tata Island beach. *Margaret Shaen. Probably 6 Jan 1898.*

year when Dolla went to Europe to study art. Over the next three years Dolla spent much of her time in artists' colonies on the continent, often in the company of well-known New Zealand artist, Frances Hodgkins.[1] Dolla also made several trips to visit Connie in Scotland and was joined by Connie in the south of France for some months in 1901.

Alla's concern for her sister relates in part to the intensity of the relationship between Connie and Dolla as well as to the fact that by 1901 Connie had developed consumption.

Alla continues:

> ... for Connie's own sake you must keep yourself in hand – I think you could not go a better way to work to kill her than by running risks like that yourself – it would be horrible for her to think she had passed this deadly thing onto you, whom she loves – I love you to have a friend yet I feel infinitely happier for you when you are away with Miss Hodgkins – it seems a healthier, saner, more manly life – even if you do get thin ...

When Connie's long-term friend, Margaret Shaen, had accompanied Connie to New Zealand she had inevitably fretted over the developing relationship with Dolla. After Dolla later turned up in Scotland, Margaret's undoubted jealousy prompted the 'tell-tale' letter to Alla. However, Dolla also wrote to Alla, pleading her and Connie's case, and putting Margaret's concerns into a more balanced context. By March the following year the tone of Alla's letters had changed.

> I am sorry you have all been making one another unhappy ... I can quite see that it was rather tragic for poor M.J.S. [Margaret], but I feel too that she doesn't take things as simply as we like to – it would solve the difficulty if one of you three would turn into a man ... I don't see why you should not all love one another as you can't help it, without taking any notice of what the third person is doing. I feel really as if C.A.A. [Constance]'s love for you was more that of a lover than her equally strong but less exciting love for M.J.S. But Margaret feels more of a lover's love for Connie and that makes it a pain to her to see her give out to you what

[1] Frances Hodgkins, the leading New Zealand woman painter of the early twentieth century.

she does not give to her ... also I think Margaret does not realize that it is better to live a full life and a short one than an empty one and a long one ... what Margaret seems aiming at when she says it tires C. to have you, or to draw or to write – let it tire her – it is life to the spirit of her ... a feverish friendship does unfit you for daily work and of course I am quite against your coming into such personal contact as is physically harmful with Connie when she is ill, but otherwise I can't see how your being together can be anything but good and a pleasure – At any rate you are as good as gold and Connie is a gem ...

A gentlewoman of impeccable pedigree, Connie Astley was descended from a long line of English landed gentry, documented back as far as one Sir Thomas Astley in 1520. The family prospered through the centuries, fortunes considerably helped when the Astleys' estate at Dukinfield became part of a prosperous mining area. Connie's parents also had a house in London and in 1851, the year Connie was born, they bought Arisaig Estate in the north-west of Scotland.

The second of four children, Connie was brought up in comfortable style, educated by the best of private tutors in an upper-class and intellectually stimulating milieu. The Astleys' circle included many of the leading thinkers of the day: socialists, Utopians and humanitarians such as William Morris and his Pre-Raphaelite group were all well known to them. They were also close to leading Unitarians William Shaen and his family. William's daughter, Margaret, was one of Connie's dearest friends.

The idyll of this privileged life was shattered in 1862 when Connie's mother died of a bronchial illness. This sad loss was followed by her father's premature death six years later. The younger Astley children were cared for by London friends and relations but the seventeen-year-old Connie and her older sister Gertrude were now generally independent, already part of London 'high society'. Money was never a significant concern as the wealthy Astley estates provided generously for all the children.

While Connie and Gertrude undoubtedly enjoyed the fun of the London social whirl, they were by no means frivolous society ladies. Highly intelligent, well-educated and imbued with a strong sense of social responsibility, they worked hard to continue their education (in the Classics, mathematics, literature, languages and science) as well as taking on activities that many of their contemporaries would never have dreamed of. Their social conscience prompted them to sponsor a ward at the workhouse near their home in London. This was not just a matter of handing over the money and then dancing into the sunset – Connie and Gertrude were regular visitors to the workhouse. Connie also went to art classes several times a week and became a member of a Bach choir that performed throughout England.

A valuable insight into their lives is given by extracts from their joint journal, which is written as if by a third person.

LONDON February 18th 1873
Mr Wilson is very particular this morning and insists on their sitting up straight and not fiddling with any thing. The proposition is rather a trial but the Latin goes pretty well. C goes to the evening class at the SKM [art school] ... In the evening they go to a ball at Mrs Eric Smith's. It is a charming house with all the rooms on the ground floor. The floor is delicious but there are too many girls and G and C get very little dancing ...

February 19th 1873
It is quite impossible to tell what time it is by the light as there is none except artificial. The gas is lighted all morning. In the afternoon G picks up C at the SKM and they go on to the Workhouse. They read and converse there diligently for about an hour and then return ... about 10.45 ... they go on to Mrs George Smith's dance. They begin dancing the moment they get there and dance nearly everything. G is introduced to Browning and feels it is an era in her life and that the anniversary ought to be kept as a high day and holiday ever after. Trollope, Du Mourier, 'John Halifax' and all sorts of grandees are there ... there are lots of pretty people and everything is delicious. They return home in a most blissful state of mind about 2.30.

Both Connie and Gertrude were actively involved in educational issues, each taking a particular interest in promoting the education of women. Especially conscious of their social responsibilities, the sisters paid to develop schools at the family estates in Dukinfield and Arisaig. They were avid followers of current events and very politically aware and, although not actively involved in the suffragette movement, they were enthusiastic supporters of women's suffrage.

April 30th 1873
G went to the House [Houses of Parliament] at 12 and remained till 6 listening to the debate on the Women's Suffrage Bill which was very interesting. Mr Fawcett made a splendid speech. They gained 12 votes more than last year but were beaten by a considerable majority.

Gertrude and Connie were also enthusiasts when it came to outdoor pursuits. They loved fishing for salmon and trout and, as Connie's editor Jill de Fresnes points out, they were the only women to appear in an active role in the game books of neighbouring Highland estates. Although Connie was probably the more energetic, both women would regularly walk sixteen or eighteen miles over the hills to visit friends, apparently unbothered by the impractical skirts and petticoats that were the order of the day. They would often accompany friends, but if none were available Connie would happily venture out for hours by herself, revelling in the glorious solitude.

1883 was a year of both sorrow and rejoicing for the Astley family: tragedy when Connie's brother Frank died in Canada, reputedly killed when he plunged over Niagara Falls in a barrel (the official report differs somewhat – it states that Frank drowned when his canoe capsized in a river); then celebrations when, at the age of thirty-three, Gertrude married Arthur Nicholson. Connie now made her permanent home with Gertrude and her family in Arisaig.

Connie's apparently boundless energies were channelled into helping the tenantry on and around the family estate. She established a carving class that was largely attended by the local men – this was sufficiently successful to be taken to a number of industrial exhibitions. In addition Connie initiated a 'Highland Home Industry', set up to enable local women to make some extra money. Typically, Connie provided spinning wheels for those who couldn't afford to buy their own and supported some of the young girls as full-time weavers. She also obtained orders for the cloth and tweed that the women would then supply.

Connie was always an enthusiastic traveller – she and Gertrude toured extensively in Europe before Gertrude's marriage and in subsequent years Connie travelled with a variety of other family members and friends. One particularly close companion was Margaret Shaen, daughter of her father's great friend, well-known lawyer and leading liberal non-conformist William Shaen. Like Connie, Margaret was highly intelligent and well educated. Deeply religious, she was a staunch Unitarian as well as being a member of the Temperance Movement. She is likely to have been a steady and serious companion, but rather lacking in the *joie de vivre* so evident in Connie.

In 1897 Connie, now aged forty-six, travelled to New Zealand with Margaret. The Shaens had close ties with the prominent Richmond and Atkinson families in New Zealand, connections begun through their shared Unitarian beliefs and continued through the generations as family members from both sides of the world visited each other.

During their travels around New Zealand Connie and Margaret stayed with many New Zealand friends, sharing their holidays and adventures. They were tourists of the most privileged sort, travelling first class whenever it was available and often staying privately, receiving the warmest of welcomes in gracious houses.

Wellington was the first port of call, briefly visited before an overnight sail to Nelson quickly followed by another to Totaranui in Golden Bay. This was a great highlight, a summer escape *en famille* at the holiday home of the Fell family. Life here was a far cry from the confines of traditional English society. At Totaranui holiday living was relaxed and communal, there was freedom of expression, a refreshing lack of respect for convention and, perhaps best of all, practical clothes were worn! Connie reports: 'Mrs F. looking active and handsome in rational costume …[2] The youngest girl, Sylvia, is a delightful little creature, dressed in very short red knicks and blue tunic trimmed with red, no shoes or stockings …' Such states of undress and no one seemed to mind! Connie writes about one visitor to the bay who couldn't adapt so easily. He '… walks about in trousers and boots, and I assure you he presents quite a shocking appearance. I have run a large tuck in my red and blue Arisaig

[2] During the 1890s the Rational Dress Association campaigned for more practical women's clothing, but with little real success. The modernisation of women's clothing had to wait until World War 1.

The Fells' house at Totaranui. *Margaret Shaen. 5 Jan 1898.*

Petticoat in order to be more fashionable.'

Eleven idyllic days were spent at Totaranui. Constance and her companions played on the sands, gathered shells, sketched on the beach, pottered around in boats, went whitebaiting in the lagoon, scrambled over rocks and hills alike. They cooked: 'We got back and set to work to cook the fish and fry the potatoes, and had a splendid dinner, with gooseberry jelly and marmalade to follow.' They boiled pipis (little shellfish) and ate them with potatoes cooked in 'an incipient bush fire'. Then there was the bonfire on the beach 'round which we all sat and had songs and choruses and recitations and chocolates, with the full moon looking down reproachfully on the bonfire, and then back to biscuits and milk.'

Their hosts were quite delightful, Mr Fell 'quite the nicest man I ever met'. This paragon not only took first-rate photographs, but, as Connie exclaims, 'he also makes the family jam'! When Connie left for Wellington, she wrote: 'I draw a veil over my feelings at leaving this enchanting place and delightful people. I was only supported by a fond and I fear delusive

At the rock on Totaranui Beach. *Margaret Shaen. 9 Jan 1898.*

Top: **Expedition to Awaroa on the Isis.** *Margaret Shaen. 6 Jan 1898.*
F-178492-1/2, CONSTANCE ASTLEY JOURNAL, DE FRESNES COLLECTION. ALEXANDER TURNBULL LIBRARY, WELLINGTON.

Bottom: **Lagoon at Totaranui, with the Dead Horse and three canoes.** *Margaret Shaen. 12 Jan 1898.*
F-178497-1/2, CONSTANCE ASTLEY JOURNAL, DE FRESNES COLLECTION, ALEXANDER TURNBULL LIBRARY, WELLINGTON.

The *Duco* at sea. *Margaret Shaen. 20 Jan 1898.*
F-178506-1/2, CONSTANCE ASTLEY
JOURNAL, DE FRESNES COLLECTION,
ALEXANDER TURNBULL LIBRARY,
WELLINGTON.

hope of a cruise at Easter, to which this angelic couple have invited me, – the invitation will anyhow remain a consolation, as I think it shows that they realize how immensely I have enjoyed myself ...' Connie especially appreciated the feeling the Fells gave her 'of complete harmony and happiness, and being in the right place'.

At Totaranui Connie had sketched determinedly, even in the most trying of conditions. When a 'furious wind' was stirring sea and sand 'my sketch got completely plastered with sand, dusty bits of fern etc, etc and my palette ditto, which spoilt my temper if not the sketch'. Sketching was by no means dependent on the time or day – any waking hour would do. A dawn departure from Picton en route back to Wellington inspired Connie to sketch 'a most peaceful scene, the sea quite calm with faint tinges of colour in it from the sky, on the left a fine barque with a little steamer towing the ship, but so silently that it seemed like a piece of nature.' This self-same steamer, the tug *Duco*, was one of two that had to rescue Connie's ferry from Cook Strait some hours later after its propeller shaft broke.

The windiness of New Zealand weather is a recurring theme in Connie's diary. Wellington, of course, gave much to comment on: 'It was as usual blowing furiously, it never does anything else at Wellington, but fortunately the wind was fair.' Even in Dunedin it was 'Blowing like mad, which it will save trouble to assume is always the case unless I say to the contrary ...'

From Wellington Connie and Margaret progressed to the deep south for what was going to be the biggest adventure of their trip – a voyage to Fiordland. Fortunately both women were good sailors, as the seas were stormy and the good ship *Waikare* rather too prone to roll when the sea was abeam.

'There is no cargo on board, which of course makes her worse, but she was very steady when head to sea and only took on one green one which sent several of us who were in the waist, ignominiously flying astern.' Connie wryly notes, 'Lunch was very poorly attended.'

Conditions improved when they entered the fiords. Connie writes in awe: 'It was very impressive to stand at the bows while the great ship forged slowly and silently ahead, penetrating deeper and deeper into the heart of these solitudes ... We are now anchored at the extreme end of this inlet, not a ripple stirring the black glassy water.'

Impressive it might have been, but it was a distinctly chilly splendour:

It has rained almost continuously and I can only compare the damp and cold to our worst experiences ... I have got a cold fit on, and I am quite sure that my 'temper' [temperature] ... is about 92. I wear an inconceivable amount of clothes and eat 7 or 8 meals per diem, and still I perish.

The fiords were not just grand, they also charmed with their luxuriance, abundance of ferns and moss, the birds and waterfalls. Boats took parties ashore to explore and have tea on the beach and the young ladies practised for a regatta. This was held in George Sound and Connie was persuaded to take an oar in one of the ladies' crews. An entertaining spectacle, but one quickly upstaged as the Second Officer, 'a very stout jovial personage, had taken out a crew of mermaids attired in bonnets and veils etc which caused much mirth during the Regatta. They had medals in the shape of ship's biscuits hung with ribbon.'

Other entertainment came from 'a very good male professional Quartette' and, on one evening, a shipboard ball with accompanying pyrotechnics:

At 9.45 there was a grand display of fireworks, varied by the firing of cannon. The reverberation amongst the mountains was something extraordinary and the effect of the rockets very fine indeed ... the dancing has now been resumed overhead, making the Music saloon where I write spring in a remarkable manner.

Milford Sound made everyone stand in awe. '... simply stupendous. Imagine mountains 5 and 6000ft high coming sheer down precipitously into the sea gorge, which is so narrow that they seem to tower over one's head, and almost overhang in one place.' The party embarked in boats and landed, catching trout and finding ferns before returning to the beach:

> When we got back we found lunch going on, everything nicely prepared by the sailors and 'billies' boiling over a cheerful fire. We were told that the Launch would not come for us till 4 and I sat down to sketch in a strong wind which defeated the sandflies just eno' to make it possible. When the wind lulled there was a buzz like 80 beehives ...

Sandflies or not, Connie had high praise when leaving Milford Sound:

> I do not think that anything could be better organised than these trips, and though everything necessary is provided there is no herding, or abominable guides, and certainly our fellow passengers were not only harmless, but many of them pleasant and interesting; still it is impossible to escape the atmosphere of a sort of almighty picnic ...

Back to Bluff: limited in appeal, but 'really not unbearably cold in all our winter clothes ... As to its lack of attractions, what can a place want where oysters are 3d. a dozen.' From here they took the train to Lumsden and then travelled on to Te Anau by coach. Connie and Margaret secured the box seat: undoubtedly lacking in traditional comforts, but marvellous for appreciating the countryside. The road was rough, the temperature distinctly cool: 'Very often it was nothing but wheel tracks, and sometimes the high tussocks brushed the pole ... Mercifully the wind had gone down, and we kept the cold out with the help of plaids, rugs, macintoshes, capes, shawls etc, etc and arrived there about 8, just as it was getting dark.'

The trip on Lake Te Anau provided somewhat more adventure than they had bargained for. Their launch was a bad start. 'Anything more ill-found, decayed, dirty or dilapidated than the appearance of the "Ripple" it would be impossible to imagine and under the most favourable circumstances she might possibly steam 6 miles an hour.' Skippered by the good Mr Snodgrass, and crewed by Jack the Engineer and Stoker, they headed off to spend the night at the far end of the lake, some fifty miles away. All went reasonably well until the last ten miles when they had to stop to refuel. This was no simple matter as Mr Snodgrass had to land and chop wood while his passengers sat and shivered in the rain. Conditions may have been trying but spirits were still high.

> One of the gentlemen came aft with the Billy full of tea and we all had some and felt more cheerful … and off we started again … and saw the great mountains at the head more and more plainly, and still it rained, yea poured, on our devoted heads, and I began to get very cheerful and sang songs … and we passed close to a beautiful wooded promontory and then we were told we were only 1/4 a mile off the head, and then it rained omnibuses and steam rollers, and blew in little squalls …

They landed at last, wet through and miserable, only to be told that they had another mile to walk before they found the accommodation house. In the gathering gloom and pouring rain, they followed the river until confronted by an uncrossable torrent. Their only option was to return to the beach. Once there the gentlemen set off to find a government hut on the other side of the river while the ladies resigned themselves to sleeping in the far-from-water-tight launch.

There was huge relief in the morning when they finally found the elusive accommodation house, a charming haven with colourful flower beds and a good wood fire. Connie also notes with relief that the condensed milk 'was much less objectionable than what I have tasted before'. There was only one real problem – the vicious attacks of countless sandflies. By the time they got back on the *Ripple* the following day, Margaret's hands were so swollen that she could hardly get her sleeves over them. Connie was so badly bitten that she looked as if she had sprained her wrist.

More adventures were to be had at Queenstown before the travellers headed north for an alpine interlude. There was some excitement en route when their coach passed the party of 'his Excellency Lord Ranfurly' returning from Mount Cook. The occasion was memorable for dust rather than glamour – the members of the viceregal party were entirely unrecognisable. One of the party, either in or on the coach, was another 'lady traveller' – Lady Ranfurly was returning from some weeks of sketching and exploring around the Alps.

> We passed a waggon drawn by a team of 6 bullocks, and I think two

waggons drawn by horses, and that was all the traffic we saw in 50 odd miles, bar his Excellency's coach ... which actually went off the road for us to pass! There were five of them outside beside the driver, and so begrimed were they by dust, that they might all have been Maoris. As for the driver, I have never seen a human being's face so caked as his was; it looked like a solid brown crust. I fancy the wind had been much higher and in their faces, for we were not incommoded at all.

Mount Cook certainly met all expectations, moving Connie to uncharacteristically purple prose:

> Dinner was at six, and afterwards we just caught the sunset glow on Mount Cook ... I went a little further and sat on a little hillock gazing ... at this pale and awful monument, the very type and image of death, dominating everything; and then came the ineffably mysterious change, and it was again luminous, not ruddy, glowing, but as it were spiritualized and transfigured, and the sky became more transparent and let the stars shine through, and the silence seemed to utter itself in a great sound of waters or a rushing wind, and night fell.

During their time at Mount Cook Margaret and Connie explored at happy length. A walk up towards the Hooker Glacier was notable not just for 'a lot of jolly new flowers and things', but also for the bridge across the Hooker River.

> The most uncomfortable bridge I was ever on. It is a suspension bridge about 80 yds. long I should think, the roadway consisting mostly of a single plank, very narrow, you have nothing to hold on to but a very loose iron wire on one side, and the whole thing wobbles and sways both laterally and perpendicularly in the most discomposing manner. As you have to look at your feet, you cannot avoid seeing the river swirling some 20 or 30 ft. below you, ugh –, also the planks in some places seemed to have a list on.

They also went on a 'perfectly heavenly expedition up to the Ball hut', where they rode horses, wore goggles against the sun and 'botanized'. Ever a keen

Constance Astley and Margaret Shaen on Tasman Glacier.

plantswoman, Connie noted the 'mountain lily, which has great leaves with a thick stalk in the centre so tough that one can haul oneself up by it ... Then 'Spaniards', with very sharp pointed stiff leaves – said to be poisonous – and great tall stems with insignificant flowers and yellow seeds and great long spines sticking out in all directions; I think Tartars would be a better name.'

They rose at 5 a.m. the following morning, breakfasted sumptuously on sardines, cocoa, coffee and gooseberry jam and set off to Tasman Glacier, an expedition well recorded by Margaret's camera. 'I do think this must be the climax of our experiences, and our luck in the weather was phenomenal.'

A tour of the North Island came next. This included a cruise up the Wanganui River where Connie was intrigued by all the Maori she saw, complete with canoes. Then it was back on a coach, up through 'great Maori country' around Raetihi. Wherever they went they were well looked after. Connie notes: 'It really is surprizing the way they feed you at these primitive little places ... It is the custom in these parts, where there are no horrible telegraph posts, to take carrier pigeons along on the coaches, to let the hotels know how many to expect ...'

The two women bathed in hot pools at Taupo, explored the thermal areas of Wairakei, and wondered at great geysers and pools of boiling mud. All impressive and a fitting foretaste of more thermal wonders to come at Rotorua. Typically, Connie was intrigued by more than the conventional attractions. Speaking of the thermal delights of Tikiteri, she writes:

> The place had a sort of unholy fascination, but time was limited and we returned to the guide's 'whare', to partake of a cup of tea! the teapot having been previously placed in a pit of boiling water just outside the door. The tea did not taste of sulphur.

When visiting the thermal area at Wai-o-tapu they were shown the area devastated by the Mount Tarawera eruption some twelve years before in 1886.

> We had a good view of the great cleft in the Tarawera Mountain, about 5 miles off, and a great region of desolation ... Talking of the eruption, there is an old woman called Sophia, who did our washing at the Geyser Hotel, whose 'whare' was the only house at Wairoa that escaped destruction and lots of people took refuge in it. She is a very striking person, with very bright intelligent eyes and most dignified carriage. It was curious to hear her talk about it. She gave me the impression that it had been a most interesting experience to her, and did not speak of it with any horror or awe.

At Huntly Connie and Margaret attended a great Maori gathering. 'They say there will never be such a gathering of Maoris again ... I must say the Maoris make a most favourable impression upon one, and it is sad to think that they are dying out.' Accommodation was a little quaint. 'This is nothing but a little township with two hotels kept by the same man, in one of which we sleep and eat in the other.' They crossed the Waikato River 'in a ferry-boat worked by a wire, or rather by the current in combination with a wire' and reached the Maori encampment. A highlight was when they persuaded the 'Natives to ferry us across' the river in a canoe.

Connie was an enthusiastic collector of rock specimens, especially volcanic rocks and in Auckland pursued this interest: '… went in again to the museum this afternoon, and have discovered a very nice name which will do I think for a large proportion of my volcanic specimens, viz: "Silicious Sinter".'

Connie sketched wherever they went, while Margaret recorded places and events with the lens. This was not always plain sailing. In Wellington Connie notes:

A terrible Tragedy in connection with M.'s photos. Owing to a mistake in working her 'changing box' she took 3 dozen on the same plate. 'Ce serait trés risible si ce n'était pas si triste.' It is really a calamity. It only affects the small ones fortunately, but there are all sorts of interesting things which can never be got again.

At Easter Margaret went to stay with family friends while Constance returned to Nelson to join the Fells for a cruise on their yacht, the *Isis*. And it was here that Connie first met 'Dolla', the beautiful thirty-seven-year-old painter, Dorothy Richmond. Connie was charmed from the outset.

I found to my joy that Miss Dorothy Richmond was coming on the cruise, and she, Mrs F. and I proceeded down to a boat-shed by the sea, and sat there in bright moonlight … waiting for Mr F. and wondering where we could possibly get to in a glass calm.

Set off they did. The days passed by most happily. They went to bed by midnight, anchored in any bay that took their fancy, landed and sketched early in the mornings and breakfasted on such treats as 'a most delicious repast of sausages and tomatoes', all cooked by their multi-talented host. They

Constance Astley, Dorothy Richmond and Mrs Fell at Sandfly Bay. *1898.*

sailed on, bathed, lunched and sailed and explored some more. Mrs Fell once again converted 'her skirt into a rational dress by sewing it up with Flax'.

They ate oysters gathered from the shore and one night Mr Fell 'cooked us a sumptuous dinner, which consisted of Huitres au naturel, Purée de Pois, Boeuf froid, tomatoes, Peaches, Apples, Cape Gooseberry jam, Plain and Beurre, Cake, Biscuits etc.' Then, they 'retired to bed in a much more complete manner about 7 p.m. D.R. on the floor, which she declared preferable to a downy couch if shared with C.C.A. It blew hard at night and rained, but nobody minded.'

Connie writes lyrically of the 'heavenly morning' on Easter Sunday when they weighed anchor at about 6.30 a.m., found another anchorage, had their 'usual delightful bathe and Toilette party … and returned on board to a tremendous breakfast' before rowing off to explore the shore. Dolla and Connie were always landed to sketch where they wished while Mr Fell acted as their 'incomparable Cook-Skipper-Mate-Steward', ensuring that they explored and ate with equal enthusiasm. The three ladies seemed to have little to do other than enjoy themselves.

Constance and Dolla often sketched and walked together, strongly drawn to each other's company. The weather was clear and warm, the surroundings superb and, when they went out in the boat at night, the scene was pure perfection: 'It was a most heavenly night, glass calm, with lots of phosphorescence, and the stars quite splendid' – a magical setting for a developing romance.

Constance was delighted when they were becalmed on the way back to Nelson – she was in no hurry to end this holiday idyll. Another night on board the yacht was a welcome bonus:

> There was a most lovely sunset, first the pink and lilac glow on the hills, turning to dark blue as the glow mounted into the sky, and reflected itself in a thousand colours on the sea. A light air which did not seem to ruffle the water at all, filled the sails and kept the yacht gliding along in perfect silence, D.R. and I went out in the boat and rowed along a little distance off, keeping the pace easily with the yacht, which looked like a beautiful phantom, silhouetted against the sky and watched by myriads of stars. It seemed a sin to waste any of these perfect hours in sleep.

Once they got back to Nelson they had to connect almost immediately with their Wellington boat, and sadly took leave of their generous hosts, the Fells.

> Still it was something to have the pang of parting from them abridged and I had the great consolation of D.R.'s sweet company. (Have you grasped that she is the daughter of Mr. James Richmond, of whose drawings I have often spoken, and who died while we were at Nelson before? She has the most beautiful grey eyes and one of the sweetest faces I have ever seen. She is going to take a studio in Wellington and devote herself to Art, but is first going to Otaki for a week or so.)

From Wellington, Connie and Dolla travelled up to Otaki to stay with Dolla's sister Alla Atkinson and all her family and here they also met up again with Margaret Shaen. The house was 'described by some one as exactly like a Chinese nunnery! is square, with a jolly wide verandah right round both ground floor and first story, and stands on a sort of plain, with a great deal of Flax and Toi-toi around it, and with sand-hills between it and the sea …' Connie continued to spend as much time as she could with Dolla.

> We had a lovely turn at the sketches before lunch; afterwards repose; – we intended to drive to the bush, but it was too wet, and D.R. and I only got a short turn along the shore. It looked very fine, the sky blue black with reddish gleams of light over a palish green sea, rolling in white breakers on the flat shore. It is a place that makes me long to sketch, and I don't know how to tear myself away either from it or the people.

Connie found her departure after the weekend very painful.

> Just hated going. D.R. is coming to Wellington on Friday or Saturday, to live with a married brother and work at Art. I wish she would have taken more rest first, She must be terribly worn out by the years of constant attendance upon her poor father, who was more helpless than a child at last.

Four days later: 'Have received a most delicious letter-card from Dolla, who arrives tomorrow.' Although she did arrive on the Saturday, time together was now limited. Dolla's brother Wilson was suddenly taken ill and she dutifully spent most of her time by his side. 'I took my Venetian photos to show her, but there seemed to be a constant succession of female visitors, which was not favourable to peaceful intercourse. I stayed an unconscionable time.'

Wilson continued to be very ill, but on the Tuesday Constance 'proceeded to keep an appointment made by telephone with Dolla, and got her to come and sit just outside the house for a little fresh air … She was still very anxious and had been in constant attendance since 7 a.m.' Fleeting visits were made to Dolla over the next couple of days. Connie was deeply fond of all the family but there is no doubt that it was Dolla she really wanted to see.

Connie and Margaret now packed their bags for the long voyage back to England. After their luggage was taken on board the R.M.S *Aorangi* on April 28 1898 there was time for one last round of visits and sad farewells to their New Zealand friends before the ship set sail the following day. Once on board Connie writes sadly:

The sun has set and we are looking our last at New Zealand. How fond I have become of it in 4 months! It has only one fault, and that is that it is so far from England, and there are such a terrible number of people in it that I want to see again. After taking the luggage on board yesterday and doing various things in Town, I found there was just time to go up and see Dolla before lunch …

Then, once on the boat:

We were so exhausted by our exertions and emotions that we remained in a state of coma in the Music room after dinner. I tried to compose poetry, but could only think of rhubarb-tart (which we had for dinner) as a rhyme to heart! so gave it up.

Although Connie's diary gives no hint of the intensity of the relationship that had developed with Dolla, the later letter from Alla made it very clear that the closeness of the bond between the two women had caused Dolla's family significant concern on the New Zealand trip.

We do not hear Connie's voice on the matter until the correspondence between Scotland and New Zealand some three or four years later when Dolla had travelled to Europe to study painting and was spending time with Connie at Arisaig.

Jealous and understandably upset, Margaret Shaen wrote not only to Alla, but also to her friend Mary Richmond, Dolla's cousin, giving them both details of the relationship between Dolla and Connie. While Alla penned a plea to Dolla, Mary immediately sent a letter to Connie, begging her to consider not just Dolla, but the family as well. Connie replied in defensive vein:

Your remarks go to my heart and of course I understand – but – well it is a strange world you are recommending – the very course against which my conscience seemed to be moving me.

I, of all people to be taking possession of and monopolizing that beautiful heavenly creature? and my only right of claim being that her eyes met mine just then – she who has the world of hearts to choose from? …

Meantime she is not here but there, and that is not true either for she has been present with me ever since that day when I had to leave her in that anguish of suspense, and a glimmer of all too soon extinguished hope, and whether she comes or not, we grow daily nearer.

Should we never meet again I ought perhaps to rejoice, that I should seem then to her like the 'far hills' which, as the Proverb has it, are the 'blue ones'. At any rate the 'golden bond' can stretch the world's width without snapping and I cannot choose but hold her in my heart …

It is hardly surprising that Margaret Shaen was jealous of the passionate relationship that had developed between Connie and Dolla. Although the exact nature of the friendship between Margaret and Connie is not entirely clear, they had certainly planned to move into a house together on their return from New Zealand. This house, Faire na Scuir, was on the Arisaig Estate. Now that Connie appeared so attached to Dolla these plans were inevitably under threat.

And it was not just Margaret who was concerned about the intensity of the relationship between Dolla and Connie. Dolla's New Zealand compatriot and painting companion, Frances Hodgkins, certainly adored Dolla or 'Miss Richmond' and may well have been in love with her. In a letter from Caudebec en Caux in August 1901 Frances writes:

Miss Richmond has decided not to go to England so we shall not lose sight of each other even for a few weeks. I have grown so fond of her, I don't know how I am ever going to let her go, she is one of those people whom you want always with you. This kind of existence is too too happy to last.

And a few days later:

Miss Richmond goes to England today, it is very sad saying goodbye to a face like hers even for a short time, I wish you could see her as she looks sometimes at night with a black dress with a crimson fichu falling off her shoulders and corals and a suggestion of old lace at her throat – I discovered it one day when she was rummaging in her boxes and have since insisted on her wearing it every night … did I tell you the girls call her the 'Divine Lady', but my dear divinity is the most human person I have ever known with an adorable sense of humor and perfect appreciation of other people's shortcomings.

Connie's visit to the painters in the south of France is a welcome diversion, with no hint of any love triangle.

29 October 1901: Miss R.s friend Miss Astley stayed with us for 10 days during which I gave her sketching lessons. She is very delicate and has to spend the winter abroad … We are to join her at her villa in San Remo on the 15th and give her more sketching lessons. She sends pathetic post-cards for me to come to her rescue as soon as possible and save her from committing any more artistic atrocities.

However, after Connie has returned to Scotland, Dolla's love and concern for Connie start to cause Frances some concern. Frances hates it when Dolla leaves her to visit Connie in Scotland, writing in a letter to New Zealand 'Miss Richmond is still in Scotland – nursing her sick friend Miss Astley … It is horrid without her.'

She also writes to Dolla in jealous style, expressing her feelings at least in part, making her point while trying to lighten sensitive issues with an amusing turn of phrase. Although talk of personal import is always buried among less intense chat, heartache is discerned behind the determinedly positive tone.

Dearest Miss Richmond

Just a line to greet you before you leave London. Are you really coming on the 4th. It seems too good to be true. I was indeed sorry to hear of the return of Miss Astley's trouble … It does not look as if Scotland was quite the best place for her does it? Please give her my love when you write or if you are with her still and tell her I didn't in the least grudge you to her. At first I felt a little furious and thought if I wrote to you at all I should begin it with a d—n then I had thought of hurling an ultimatum at your head – and then of a warrant for your arrest and forcible abduction but slept over it and calmed down and decided to let matters take their own course … I moved in here last Monday – and am most comfortable but lonely – and I shall be very glad when I shall have you sitting opposite me again at meals

[continues in cheerful and chatty vein].

Another letter, written to Dolla in March 1903, makes it very clear that Frances knows that she comes a poor second to Connie in Dolla's affection. Dolla has written in praise of Frances's letters. Frances replies:

> … I am really terribly proud to think you like them – how do they compare with Miss Astley's for instance – but of course I know that you wld rather nurse one of her empty envelopes than read the outpourings of my innermost soul – however I mustn't expect too much.

Writing some years before the letters detailing the relationship between Connie and Dolla came to light, Linda Gill, editor of Frances Hodgkins' letters, notes:

> It will probably never be known whether Frances Hodgkins was absolutely the celibate woman she appears to be. There are no love letters in the conventional sense of the term. Her brief engagement to the writer Thomas Wilby remains mysterious … What does emerge from the letters is her passionate delight in the beauty of women and her enjoyment of the company of intelligent, well-informed and adventurous people, men and women. Whether these emotions were ever given sexual expression is less important than the fact that they were experienced with such pleasurable intensity. In Dorothy Richmond she found a person who combined many of the qualities she admired, and the time spent painting with her in France and Italy was the most exuberantly happy period of her life. She wrote of and to Miss Richmond in the language of love, a usage sanctioned by the tradition of romantic friendship between women, and not necessarily indicative of any closer relationship.

If she had known of the intensity of the love affair between Connie and Dolla, Linda Gill may have drawn a different conclusion.

After 1902 we hear little of Connie. Although we know that Dolla was still treasuring her letters a year later, Connie abruptly stopped writing her diaries in 1902. There is no indication of what prompted her to do so after avidly recording daily events for over thirty years. Maybe life just became too repetitive, maybe she was feeling too ill. It is probably significant that one of the last pages contains a postcard from Dolla, sent from Land's End.

Although Connie's consumption was obviously of great concern at the time of Dolla's visit, she appears to have recovered well – certainly she survived to live a full life and achieve a respected old age. Connie spent the rest of her life at Arisaig, ever a pillar of the community, a great force behind the founding of the local Women's Rural Institute and very involved in organising the war effort. Margaret Shaen continued to be a close friend and, as such, spent several months of every year with Connie at Faire na Scuir. However, she never made her permanent home with Connie.

Jill de Fresnes, editor of Connie's diaries, notes that:

In company she did not know, Constance Astley was reserved. She is remembered by those who knew her when they were children as an austere, impressive but formidable old lady. In her journals between 1872 and 1902, however, she comes across as an extremely intelligent, creative, witty and outgoing character, with a tremendous appetite for life and seemingly boundless energy.

Even though Connie never met Dolla again after Dolla's return to Wellington in 1903, there is no doubt that she always retained a firm place in Connie's affections. Connie kept a portrait photograph of Dolla on one of the sitting-room tables in her house for the next thirty years or more. This gentle reminder of her beloved friend remained in pride of place until long after Connie's death, at the age of eighty-four, in 1935.

BIBLIOGRAPHY

De Fresnes, Jill (Ed), *Constance Astley's Trip to New Zealand 1897–1898*. Wellington: Victoria University Press, 1997.

Gill, Linda (Ed). *Letters of Frances Hodgkins*. Auckland: Auckland University Press, 1993.

Porter, Frances. *Born to New Zealand: A Biography of Jane Maria Atkinson*. Wellington: Bridget Williams Books, 1989.

THE RICHARDSON SISTERS

Lillie: 1868 – 1937; Ethel: 1869 – 1946; Fanny: 1872 – 1954

VICTORIAN TOMBOYS

TUESDAY 21ST 10 1890. HERE WE ARE ANCHORED LOWER DOWN IN PORT PEGASUS, AND WE SAW FOUR BIG KING PENGUINS SWIMMING CLOSE TO THE PORT HOLE IN THE SALOON, IT IS VERY VERY COLD, AND IT KEPT ON raining and hail squalls, hard, the deck was white, it is blowing a regular Sou West gale, and the glass has gone down to 28, 82, lower than it has been since 1860 ... it did blow cats and dogs, after dinner I made draught men 14 of each ... Lillie pressed moss, and practised [the violin] ... we couldn't go on deck it was blowing too hard, and it was a wild night.

On Friday 26 September 1890, three young Victorian ladies set sail from Wellington on the government steamer *Hinemoa*, bound for the sub-antarctic islands. This was no isolated voyage – these three were veterans of shipboard travel, still treasuring sketches from their Chatham Islands voyage, their 'round the North' trip a recent memory. The girls were well acquainted with the captain, a friend of their father. In fact it was the kindly captain who encouraged the trio to sail for the icy southern seas at very short notice – the girls only

The Richardson sisters: Ethel, Fanny and Lillie. *Ethel Richardson, Ship's log, 1890.*

decided to sail a few hours before the *Hinemoa* was scheduled to depart!

Lillie, Ethel and Fanny Richardson were the daughters of runholder, surveyor and politician George Frederick Richardson and his wife Lillie. These girls were of adventurous stock, their sea-going enthusiasm undoubtedly owing much to their maternal great-grandfather, an admiral in the Royal Navy.

The sisters lived their early years on the family property of 'Oaklands' in Southland, an upbringing that fostered a great love for the outdoors. Later writings show a strong appreciation for everything botanical and a great affection for all animals and birds. Horse-riding was something they were keen to do at any opportunity – in true tomboy style on their southern trip they captured two cart horses at Bluff, fashioned a bridle out of flax and took turns riding these sturdy steeds.

Shortly after their father became a minister in the Atkinson government in 1887, the girls and their two brothers were brought by their mother to join him in Wellington. The family's new-found city 'society' may have been superior to that of Southland, but these young ladies appear to have found it all a little claustrophobic. The intrepid trio seemed set on adventure at every opportunity.

The second sister, twenty-one-year-old Ethel, records the six-week sub-antarctic trip in her 'ship's log'. Written in exuberant, breathless style, her flow of consciousness-like sentences move from topic to topic, often lasting a page or more. Ethel's enthusiasm is refreshing, though a little exhausting for the reader!

Jacksons' Bay, 15 October
the moss was most beautiful in piles and piles and piles just heaps of green moss and all wet and such lovely earth for flowers and all the time the birds were singing, no wonder we were happy, no wonder we ran with young legs and light hearts, the robins were singing every where their dear little clear voices ringing out in the silent gullies … we were coming along in fine style in nickerbockers and dresses hauled up, talking at the rate of knots and there was 'Merryeanus' and Robinson; we nearly ran slap into them but our dresses were down before they saw us.

Ethel's account gives the impression of three delightful young women, each of

'S.S. "Hinemoa" 31st 10/90. I drew this in the Saloon'. *Ethel Richardson, Ship's log.*

them bursting with energy and humour. Practical jokes abounded as they passed their time flirting with shipmates, singing, dancing and fooling around. Their friends among the crew all acquired nicknames – the rationale for each of these was never explained, but 'Moondyne', 'Nimble', 'Merryeanus' (Andrew Knox, the ship's carpenter) and 'Alabastor' provided much entertainment. There was an abundance of laughter and high spirits. These were girls who often 'had grand fun, till late'.

The girls stocked up on spare violin strings and took their instruments on board. Lillie, in particular, practised most conscientiously. Other activities were invented along the way.

> I got 'Merryeanus' to get me a board from forrard and I made a draught board out of it, and some cork men, that blew away when we played on deck, so we got a potato from by the alley and made men that wouldn't blow away out of the potato, we read most of the afternoon, and Lillie went to sleep.

'Fanny after a Sea Lion on Adams Island. SUN/26/10/90.' *Ethel Richardson, Sketchbook.*

At a later point Ethel made some wooden draughtsmen and dyed them appro-priately – so much more attractive than the prospect of playing with mouldy potato pieces! She also learned a variety of nautical knots from the second mate, sketched and wrote poetry. Along with her two sisters, Ethel gaily rose to the challenge of sneaking food out of the pantry and teasing even more out of the cook. Shipboard fare was wholesome – milk (fresh from the ship's cow) the drink of choice, ham, fish, cake, plum tart and biscuits all eagerly devoured. Buckets of oysters appeared on the menu at Bluff, while rabbit stew featured after good hunting on the Auckland Islands.

In true Victorian style the girls collected all sorts of things as they went. Lillie appears to have been the most enthusiastic botanist – crew members found rare plants for her and she spent quiet moments pressing moss and ferns. All the girls gathered birds' eggs, but these collectors' items paled into insignif-icance compared with the sea lions they helped crew members bring on board

'We find the "Derry Castle" huts & crawl inside.' *Ethel Richardson, Sketchbook, 1890.*
REPRODUCED BY COURTESY OF CYNTHIA CASS.

– these were a major trophy to show to South Island friends!

Chasing sea lions was an ongoing challenge as the animals were less than tolerant. Castaway depots were safer territory, carefully inspected on every island, along with relics of actual castaways:

Saturday October 25th, 1890

… we chased … sealions into the sea … they kept coming at us; one snorted and came at Fannie and she popped away and said ('Oh! Shut up') we had grand fun after them, and ran the 3 down to the water, and we could hear them on board laughing at us. Then we went and looked at the 'Derry Castle' huts, they were made of tussock and sticks tied up with strips of sea lions skin … we went in one of the huts, you had to crawl in … just a little dump, it was so dry inside too, the 'Derry Castle' crew built the huts, 3 of them, and lived in them 22 months when they were wrecked there.

The *Hinemoa* must have seemed a veritable 'Noah's ark' as it steamed its way around the southern ocean. The ship's cow and other unfortunate beasts were unloaded as they went, part of a policy of introducing self-sustaining flocks to these forbidding islands – a source of food for future castaways. They landed a 'heffer' at the Antipodes Islands, two sheep and two goats on Campbell Island and, on the Auckland Islands, 'we took two goats an old and a young and a Southdown sheep and let them go ashore, but the poor old beggars wouldn't leave the boat and stopped on the beach by it.' The Snares were allotted more exotic livestock: goats, possums and kiwi. In return the boat was loaded with southern fauna: sea lions, scores of penguins, two albatrosses and a sea hawk.

Although Ethel's diary gives no hint of a special relationship between 'Merryeanus' and any of the girls, true love certainly blossomed after the voyage. Andrew Knox married the oldest sister, Lillie, and they moved to a sheep station in Pahiatua. They had two children. Lillie's granddaughter, Cynthia Cass, notes that 'her consuming passion was horses, and it was said she valued them above people'.

The trip's chronicler, Ethel, worked as a draughtswoman for the Department of Lands and Survey. In later years she lived in a cottage at Waiho Gorge, Mount Cook. Family tradition tells that she did this to be near the great (and eminently proper!) mountain guide, Peter Graham, whom she secretly admired. Ethel made ends meet by selling her oil and watercolour paintings to tourists at the Hermitage hotel.

Fanny remained living in Wellington and devoted her life to her art. Her experiences among the rich bird life of the southern seas are likely to have given her much inspiration for her illustrations for the *Forest and Bird* magazine. She also exhibited regularly at the Academy of Fine Arts. Cynthia Cass recalls her as 'an aunt much loved by many for her sense of humour'.

BIBLIOGRAPHY

Cass, Cynthia, 'Lillie Richardson, Ethel Richardson, Fanny Richardson.' In: MacDonald, Charlotte, Penfold, Merimeri and Williams, Bridget. *The Book of New Zealand Women, Wellington*: Bridget Williams Books, 1991.

Richardson, Ethel. *Ship's log*. Unpublished.

THE COUNTESS OF RANFURLY
1858 – 1932

The Countess of Ranfurly is one of the loveliest women we have had in Australia for a long time. The Countess has reached mellow womanhood and lost none of her more youthful beauty. Her calm, beautiful face is unwrinkled, her figure straight and finely moulded, her shoulders and arms are white as snow, her carriage 'steals a grace beyond the rules of art'. There is nothing more charming that the dignified maturity of Lady Ranfurly combined with the calm and fresh beauty of her earlier years.

These admiring lines, written on the occasion of Lord and Lady Ranfurly's visit to Melbourne in 1899, appeared in the *Melbourne Punch*. And they were no isolated words of praise. Scrapbooks kept during the six and a half years the Ranfurlys spent in New Zealand hold many more such descriptions, each one admiring of the lovely countess. When one New Zealand society page reporter notes somewhat acidly: 'There were many smart frocks and pretty women to look at, though it was not always the one who wore the other' she was most

Her Excellency, the Countess of Ranfurly. 1897.
MSZ-0827-002, RANFURLY COLLECTION, ALEXANDER TURNBULL LIBRARY, WELLINGTON.

certainly not referring to the Governor's lady. The correspondent goes on to write:

> Lady Ranfurly danced frequently, and looked well-dressed, gracious and sweetly pretty, as a Governor's wife should do, and wore a lovely gown of rose-coloured moiré velours, trimmed on the corsage and skirt with exquisite Venetian point lace, and her diamonds were viewed with envious eyes by every woman in the room.

Born in Ireland on 30 November 1858, Constance Elizabeth Caulfield was the only daughter of the seventh Viscount Charlemont and the Honourable Annetta Handcock, younger daughter of Baron Castlemaine. We know little about her upbringing, but English society pages note that she was a renowned beauty. Later articles report that she had a love of boating and sailing, and could row most competently. Her fondness for music and art was often noted. Constance married the Earl of Ranfurly, a fellow member of the Irish aristocracy, in 1880, when she was about twenty-two years old.

Uchter John Mark Knox, younger brother of the fourth Earl of Ranfurly, had been sent to sea at the tender age of fourteen, a career in the Royal Navy deemed most appropriate for an earl's second son. Then, in 1875, his elder brother died on a shooting expedition in Abyssinia and unexpectedly the young aristocrat became the fifth Earl. He was just nineteen. Once Lord Ranfurly succeeded to the title he spent some time studying at Oxford before returning to the land. His country seat was Northland House at Dungannon in County Tyrone.

Lord Ranfurly always had an adventurous and entrepreneurial streak and, before his appointment to the governorship of New Zealand, spent many years establishing extensive citrus orchards at Mildura on the Murray River, Victoria, Australia. These were largely administered from afar, but Lord Ranfurly often visited for three months at a time.

Lord Ranfurly became a Lord in Waiting to Queen Victoria in 1895, a role which meant that he was being closely considered for some position of significant responsibility. It is unlikely to have been a surprise when, in January 1897, Lord Ranfurly was offered the appointment of Governor of New Zealand.

The British press considered Ranfurly a popular choice, and described him as an 'open-hearted, frank, honest-minded Irishman' known for both his clear judgement and his capacity for hard work. At the time of his appointment he was described as 'forty-one years of age, but he looks younger, and evidences are not wanting in him of a strong and energetic temperament. He is of average height and has rather a juvenile appearance. Affability is one of his chief charms.'

The appointment was definitely seen as a step-up in life, financially as well as in terms of responsibility, status and challenge. As a Lord in Waiting, Lord Ranfurly was paid £702 a year. As the Governor of New Zealand he would be paid £5000.

Such an increase in income did not, however, promise true financial reward. One British paper reported:

> It is not everyone who can afford an Australian governorship, for it implies an expenditure of four or five thousand a year more than the official income. Lord Ranfurly, though not a rich peer, can afford this extra expenditure, and as he and Lady Ranfurly are a charming host and hostess, may expect a good time at Government House.

Such calculations were fairly close to the mark. A cash book, diligently kept by Lord Ranfurly's private secretary and aide-de-camp Dudley Alexander throughout the tour in New Zealand, gives a comprehensive summary of expenses from 1897 to 1904. We read that the initial outfit for New Zealand cost £3540, the journey to New Zealand £2156 and that the cost of wine consumed during the period was £2560. Total expenses incurred in New Zealand amounted to £57,542. The Governor's salary was raised to £7000 for some years which helped a little, but once the seven years of salary were deducted from the seven years of expenses the Earl of Ranfurly was still £21,550 out of pocket. This was certainly no post for the poor.

When the appointment was announced the Ranfurlys' son, Viscount Northland, was fourteen years old, six feet tall and already well established at Eton College. It was decided that he would stay there, but would later on miss a term and come out to see the family. At this point it was envisaged that the New Zealand appointment would be only for three years.

The Countess of Ranfurly and her youngest daughter, Lady Eileen Knox.
From a painting by Mrs Adrian Hope.

Lady Constance Knox with bicycle.

Newspaper records of the time generally refer to four children, but only give details of three. The eldest, a daughter, was born just nine months after the Ranfurlys' marriage in 1880. *Burke's Peerage* records her death five and a half years later. There is no hint as to the cause. However, there were two younger daughters who travelled to New Zealand with their parents. Lady Constance Ranfurly (Puss) was about to turn twelve, Lady Eileen was still just five. There was never any question of leaving either of the girls behind.

Packing for New Zealand was a major undertaking, especially considering that a Governor's family was expected to live, entertain and travel in significant style. None of the family horses was taken but 'four carriages, two landaus, a victoria and a waggonette' were duly packed. A buggy was to be purchased in New Zealand. And the family pet was not forgotten – Lady Ranfurly was to take her Skye terrier Hamish.

The viceregal party sailed from Liverpool on 3 June 1897 on the Royal Mail Steamer, the SS *Parisian*. Once they had crossed the Atlantic they travelled overland across Canada to Vancouver on the Canadian Pacific railway in a special car provided by the Governor of Canada. The party consisted of Lord and Lady Ranfurly, the Ladies Constance and Eileen Knox, Lord Ranfurly's private secretary and aide-de-camp, Captain Dudley Alexander, a Miss Costello, a nurse, a valet and a maid. The party spent three weeks in this carriage as they included some sightseeing in their journey – a visit to Niagara Falls was of special note. An interested press report noted that this train would carry about sixty tons of luggage belonging to the viceregal party, including four carriages, 600 cases of wine, a plentiful supply of guns and fishing tackle, several tents and all the impedimenta of a large household.

From North America the party travelled to Sydney and then on to New Zealand. They eventually arrived in Wellington by the government steamer *Tutanekai* on the morning of 10 August 1897.

The welcome was splendid. There was a procession of boats, including one of Maori in song, and the ships in the harbour were gaily decorated with bunting, blue-jacketed sailors adorning the yards of the HMS *Phylades*. Once ashore the party was met by a carriage with four horses which took them straight to the Parliament Buildings through crowded streets. However, although the arrival festivities were impressive, Government House was dismally disappointing. Lord Ranfurly wrote wryly:

Government House did not look an inviting residence, packing cases and trunks pervaded space. The decorations had decidedly lost their pristine vigour, the furniture too was past all words … Chairs with three legs were not suitable for entertaining, nor were they a credit to the Colony.

In fact things were so dire that the Ranfurlys decided not to wait for the necessary Parliamentary vote before remedying the situation, but immediately started to refurbish the residence at their own expense. Fortunately these expenses were later refunded.

One of the Earl's first duties was to officiate at the opening of Parliament. This was a grand affair necessitating full dress uniform and appropriate ceremony, and should have been a fine and solemn occasion – if only the horses had obliged. When the royal salute was fired the four horses drawing the Earl's carriage took fright and bolted: the gates of Parliament were eventually entered on the third attempt!

Early impressions of Wellington were inevitably shaped to some degree by the events of 22 September:

The earthquake came with startling suddenness. First there was a roar like the noise of a heavy wind, then a crackling sound, like that of the snapping of timbers as the earth shook … then another rumbling sound … to the accompaniment of the noise of falling bricks from chimneys, the shattering of panes of glass and the jangling of bells all over the town …

The quake lasted between twelve and fifteen seconds and proved terrifying in Wellington. Papers of the time reported in dramatic detail how 'people rushed into the streets startled almost out of their wits', while 'women fainted or went into hysterics … The men on board the ships in the Harbour, rushed on deck believing their vessels were in collision.' Strangely the viceregal party, travelling by carriage through Petone, felt nothing at all.

Before the departure for New Zealand some significant concern had been expressed in the English and Irish media as to how much Lady Ranfurly would be missed in 'Society', and even more concern as to what she could possibly do to fill her time in New Zealand. They need not have worried. The social whirl that began shortly after the Ranfurlys first arrived in the country hardly let up for the next seven years. There were balls, levees, 'At Homes', garden parties, conversaziones, official receptions and flower shows, the Governor and his Lady graciously presiding over every occasion. Football games were also important though generally of more interest to the Governor.

Lady Ranfurly worked as she socialised, and quickly involved herself in charitable societies throughout the country. She took particular interest in issues concerning women, children, animals and education, most especially that of Maori girls. The Mothers' Union, the Society for the Prevention of Cruelty to Animals and the Society for the Protection of Women and Children were all organisations that received the countess's special attention. Lady Ranfurly presided over 'At Homes' held for old soldiers of all ranks, executing with care her task of pinning the medals and ribbons onto the veterans' uniforms. And, whatever the occasion, she dressed with elegance and graciously gathered bouquets proffered by little girls in their Sunday best.

Grand social occasions were part and parcel of the Ranfurlys' life, balls a special challenge. Lord Ranfurly relates one especially memorable occasion, a fancy-dress ball in Wellington during the visit of their son Tom in 1898:

> Our balls in one respect were always a particular success, I refer to the decorations, my wife personally superintended these, taking often too active a part, resulting in her being very fatigued before the ball had commenced ...
>
> On 27 October the ball took place. Lady Ranfurly and myself were dressed as our ancestors the Rt. Hon Thos and Lady Juliana Penn (when he was Governor of Pennsylvania in its first settlement) and our children as their children, and our staff as their staff.
>
> At 9.30 ... we entered the ballroom in procession, it was a most brilliant sight, the costumes being quite equal to any that could be seen in Europe. For this ball, the invitations had been issued many months [before] so as to enable those who so desired to obtain dresses from Europe.

The ball was an undoubted success with dancing until 3.00 a.m.

It is unfortunate that we have none of Constance's letters or diaries – it would have been fascinating to have her personal account of the New Zealand years. However, much of the 'essential Constance' can be gleaned from the writing of others. The Governor's private secretary, Dudley Alexander, wrote extensive journals which give us an insight into the Ranfurlys' time here, and Lord Ranfurly wrote detailed records, often with the very obvious help of Alexander's notes! Alexander also assiduously kept scrapbooks of the whole New Zealand experience. These start at the time the earl's appointment was announced and continue for seven years until the return to England. They are full of newspaper cuttings, factual journalistic accounts of meetings and tours, photographs of the viceregal family and many, many accounts of what the family (and especially the countess) wore and the occasions they wore them to. All these contribute to a warm and gracious image of a talented First Lady.

Constance's artistic talents were ever to the fore, not only in her water-colour painting (she exhibited at the Wellington Art Exhibition in 1897) but also in the influence she had in the refurbishment of both the Wellington and Auckland Government Houses. Local society pages give her huge credit here. One Birthday Ball, held at Government House in Auckland on 8 June 1899, is described as a 'Brilliant Viceregal Function', and we are further told:

> Never in the whole history of gubernatorial entertainments in this colony has so much trouble been taken by the Viceregal host and hostess in the matter of decorations ... The Countess, who organised and supervised the whole scheme, came to us with a reputation as an artist, and most certainly we can say ... 'the half was not told us'. We all of us owe a debt of gratitude to Lady Ranfurly for refusing to come to Auckland till Government House and the entertaining rooms were properly decorated.

The writer goes on to remind readers that previously the ballroom was 'a dingy, dirty barnlike structure, with damp walls and tattered hangings'.

However, newly done-up ballrooms could have their problems. In the scrapbook for 1897–1898 we read of one less-than-successful occasion.

> There were many complaints about the floor at the previous ball given by Lady Ranfurly, as by mistake it was waxed before the first preparation was properly dry, so that many of the ladies' dresses suffered on this account,

Her Ladyship's dress being among them. The floor has since been taken up and re-laid, so that it ought to be in first-class order for tonight.

There were no reports to the contrary.

The newspaper reports consistently confirm the countess's talents: 'Lady Ranfurly is an ardent worshipper of the Goddess of Flowers, the chrysanthemum being one of her special favourites. Her hobby is arranging indoor floral decorations.' This was an especially useful art when faced with vast ballrooms and reception rooms to decorate. This would not have been a solitary task for the countess, however: she would have acted as 'artistic director' for a small army of willing helpers.

Constance was also a most able singer and musician, happy to perform to audiences of all kinds. One such occasion was an evening held at Government House for seamen of all nationalities and ranks. Those present were encouraged to smoke and generally make themselves at home before they were treated to a grand supper and concert, this last including Constance playing the piano and singing. Likewise, when the Ranfurlys spent Christmas at Waikanae, Constance played the harmonium at the local Christmas service.

The Mothers' Union also benefited from their countess's talent. At the end of one concert she sat at the pianoforte and 'sang with great feeling and sweetness an Irish melody "The Meeting of the Waters", tastefully playing for her own accompaniment'.

It was events such as these, held in conjunction with numerous tours around the country, that ensured the Ranfurlys' immense popularity with the New Zealand people. They may have been viceregal, but they were certainly never élitist when it came to entertaining. Far from restricting their guest lists to the leading lights of society and the business world, they both went to 'huge lengths to be acquainted with the country and the people'.

Constance also endeared herself to the public in the way she spontaneously involved herself in whatever had to be done. When a fire broke out near Government House she was one of the first on the scene, helped to rescue chattels from the house and spent time comforting the inhabitants. This was widely reported in the newspapers the following day.

'Governor's Special'. *Dudley Alexander's journal, 1902.*
MSY-4600-055, RANFURLY COLLECTION, ALEXANDER TURNBULL LIBRARY, WELLINGTON.

WELLINGTON, Auckland
April – May 1902

Dearest Alice -

I must write you a short account of a Railway trip we have done, I am afraid there is not much novelty about it, as most of it was over old ground I have already described. However we did some entirely new places, so it may interest you to hear about them.

R. C. self + Capt. Boscawen (Hon'. A.D.C. in Auckland + District) with a cook + boy, Butler + footman, + Allen the maid left Auckland one fine day for a run on the lines South of Auckland. We had the same kind of train as I have already described, each with his little cabin, a saloon + dining room, cooking van + luggage van, + a special engine in attendance – After a 2 hours run we got to Wairangi, a Government experimental farm. Here grapes + wattle bark are grown. It is run entirely for the good of the settlers in the Colony. There are several of these farms scattered about in different parts. After a short time we left for "Ngaruawahia" (pronounce it if you can), left the train + started with two

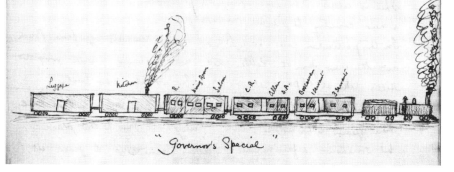

" Governor's Special "

143

Lady Ranfurly on steps of viceregal carriage. *Dudley Alexander's journal, 1902.*
MSY-4600-069, RANFURLY COLLECTION, ALEXANDER TURNBULL LIBRARY, WELLINGTON.

Much of the Ranfurlys' time was spent on viceregal tours of the country. Travel in the South Island was by steamer and coach, while the North Island was toured by train and coach, the most efficient manner of travelling throughout New Zealand at that time. They travelled with quite a party – typically there would be Lord and Lady Ranfurly, Dudley Alexander, another aide-de-camp, a cook, a 'boy', a butler and a footman. In addition there could be relevant officials or any family or friends who happened to be visiting at the time.

In his later journal Lord Ranfurly reported: 'The travelling by train was very comfortable. We had ample accommodation for sleeping, a good saloon for the daytime, besides a compartment for work, a van fitted up as a kitchen.' This kitchen had 'a tank with several hundred gallons of water, so we could have baths as needed. We had no regular bathroom, but india rubber and canvas baths are easily packed … These we had brought from home.'

After the royal visit of the Duke and Duchess of Cornwall and York, travelling through the North Island by rail got rather grander. Carriages had been built expressly for the royal tour and these were now available for the Governor's use. Restrained comfort was replaced by more opulent style. Not only were the fittings of the royal saloon of the finest red morocco leather, but there were also two good armchairs, a library chair, a table, a bookcase, a comfortable chesterfield sofa and a gas fire. There was another comfortably appointed carriage for the staff and an office for the duke's secretary to conduct his business.

These trips around New Zealand involved a gruelling schedule of official visits – to woollen mills, ostrich farms and dairy factories, coal mines, freezing works, hospitals, mental asylums and prisons. Schools and veterans' homes were ever on the agenda with Constance being particularly in demand when it came to opening flower shows.

The government steamers that took the viceregal party around the New Zealand shores would inspect and supply lighthouses on their way. This could be a risky business as the shores were often inhospitable, whaleboats only too prone to turn over in the surf. One lighthouse provided an especially interesting bounty – when the party called at Stephen's Island in the Marlborough Sounds they caught nine tuatara, primitive, large lizard-like reptiles peculiar to New Zealand. These were carefully carted back to Wellington and released in the Government House gardens. Unsurprisingly no mention is ever made of them again!

Undoubtedly the most adventurous forays were those to the sub-antarctic islands, journeys for which Lord Ranfurly had a unique brief. On the first of these he noted that '... the chief object ... is to carry out a promise I made to obtain specimens of birds for the Natural History Department, British Museum, as through the effect of time and moth, their New Zealand collection wanted largely renewing'.

When Dudley Alexander accompanied the earl on this trip he dutifully recorded the large range of birds they caught, including a black oystercatcher they 'potted' for the British Museum. He further notes the technique for ensuring such finds were properly preserved:

... have large jars and in these place fresh water with from $2^1/2$ to 5% Formaline; pop the bird whole into the jar, having first opened him below the breast bone and wrapped him up in butter cloth to prevent the

SS *Tutanekai* at Lyttelton. I January 1898.
MSZ-0827-003, RANFURLY COLLECTION, ALEXANDER TURNBULL LIBRARY, WELLINGTON.

plumage being damaged – In this manner the bird will get home, after any
length of time, as fresh as the day he was shot.

The second viceregal bird-collecting cruise to the chilly south came just a year
later. The SS *Tutanekai* set off from Wellington on 26 December 1901, bound
for the 'Southern Islands of New Zealand and the Macquarie Islands'. This
time the party included Lady Ranfurly and her daughters, Lady Constance and
Lady Eileen, along with a Miss B. Douglas (probably the girls' governess).
Notable among the other passengers was Charles Worsley, official artist for
the exhibition.

This was no joy ride – as usual the viceregal party had to fit in with the
regular duties carried out by the steamer. They visited lonely lighthouses as
they progressed down mainland New Zealand, landing stores such as coal, oil,
food, furniture and timber by whaleboat. Alexander writes: 'We crept along
doing Lighthouses.' No fair-weather visitors these – if the weather was too bad
to land supplies they had to stand by until matters improved. This was just the

beginning of the party's extra duties: during the next few weeks they would also be checking for castaways, resupplying castaway depots and loading some quite extraordinary cargo.

The *Tutanekai* briefly sheltered at Port Pegasus at the bottom of Stewart Island before heading south-west for the Snares. These islands were an inspiring first port of call. The wealth of all sorts of bird life was extraordinary, but the millions of penguins were an especially dramatic presence. Dudley Alexander noted that these strange birds 'waddle along on their two feet and have a quaint appearance. They are of no value unless boiled down in immense quantities for their oil.' Muttonbirds were also there in abundance, 'the sea and the sky were black with them.' Albatrosses were nesting; eggs were gathered by the viceregal party as curiosities to be sold at a bazaar in aid of a new convalescent home.

All the party landed on the Snares, and walked among the penguins, fur seals and sea-lions. These last could be distinctly off-putting. On the previous trip Lord Ranfurly had been attacked by a sealion 'and it was only after the second barrel that the vicious beast returned into the water'. This time his younger daughter Eileen was 'rather terrified with the lions who were roaming about and roaring'.

The next port of call was at the Auckland Islands, reached on the morning of 8 January. Here they landed at Enderby Island at a place with 'some graves of people who had died of starvation in 1864. Mr Worsley painted anew the inscription which was getting faded – This was in "Terror Cove".' It was near this point that the *Tutanekai* passed the French barque *Jean Baptista* en route from Dunkirk to Tahiti. This may have seemed a long way from its destination, but it is pointed out that in order to catch the best winds and currents, 'sailing ships always have to take the grand circle. This accounts for the many wrecks which take place on these various islands.'

Once here they also had to check the castaway depots. Dudley Alexander had described such depots the previous year.

These depôts are a fine institution for castaways and are visited about every 6 months by the 'Hinemoa' or one of the H.M.S. In large Islands like the Aucklands there are many 'depôts' dotted about some being merely a boat with directions as to how to get to the principal food depôt

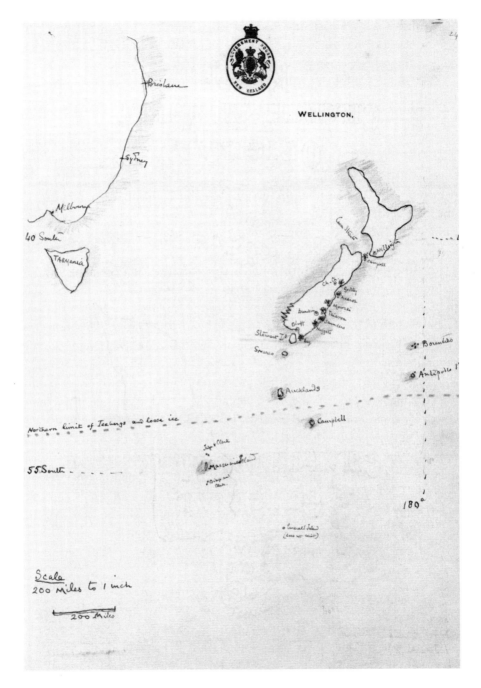

WELLINGTON,

Brisbane

Sydney

Melbourne

40 South

TASMANIA

Cook Strait

Wellington

Campbell

Ch⁰

Greiby

Akaroa

Dunedin Moeraki

Oliver Tuiaroa

Stewart I⁰ Timaru

Snares Nuggets

Bounties

Antipode I

Aucklands

Northern limit of Icebergs and loose ice

Campbell

55 South

Judge & Clerk

Macquarie Island

P. Disappoint
Cave

180°

Emerald Island
(does not exist)

Scale
200 Miles to 1 inch

200 Miles

– In these depôts are stores sufficient for about 10 men for a year – amongst other things is a gun and cartridges, also each shed has a Bible tied up in paper hung up to the rafter to prevent rats eating the paper. There is food, clothing, soap, tobacco, fishing kit, etc, etc. All these islands have depôts, and at various places one sees signposts put up to indicate to castaways the nearest way to their stores.

Enderby and the Auckland Islands behind them, they headed for Macquarie Island, some 360 miles to the south, sailing well below the 'northern limit of Icebergs and loose ice'. The following two nights and day at sea were memorably miserable. However, although the weather was awful and the temperature bitterly cold, all aboard were in remarkably good heart. Dudley Alexander notes that 'we had now got our sea legs … The rolling of the boat, when half one's dinner comes rolling over one only adds to the humour of the situation.' Nevertheless, it was an undoubted relief when calmer waters were finally reached.

Macquarie Island was a Tasmanian possession, visited chiefly because a New Zealander had leased it 'in order to procure penguin oil, which is used in some way in "doing-up" N.Z. Flax'. In pursuit of this he and his men had slaughtered millions of penguins, boiled up their carcasses to extract the oil and then burned their spent bodies as fuel to boil up yet more freshly slaughtered penguins. Although this practice had not been carried out for some years, many barrels of oil had been left on the beaches when the *Gratitude*, the schooner sent to retrieve them, was wrecked on the shore. The *Tutanekai* was tasked with picking up as many barrels as possible – on one beach they found eighty barrels of penguin oil, while in total they retrieved 204.

Millions of penguins may have been slaughtered, but there were millions more to be seen and smelt. While the king penguin was in strong evidence and greatly admired by all, the smell was another matter. 'The "spring-violet essence bouquet" was charming! It nearly did for us, luckily the wind shifted after a while.' Sea elephants were another feature of Macquarie Island. The largest ones had a sort of trunk, rather like a tapir and appeared to the visitors to be about the size of a young elephant without legs.

Map by Dudley Alexander of New Zealand's sub-antarctic islands. *Dudley Alexander's journal, 1902.*
MSY-4600-024, RANFURLY COLLECTION, ALEXANDER TURNBULL LIBRARY, WELLINGTON.

Shooting in wet weather at Macquarie Island. Dudley Alexander and Lady Ranfurly.
Dudley Alexander's journal, 1902.

Next port of call was a remarkably rough 400 miles away. 'The party retired to bed, and there they remained till we reached Campbell Island, some 53 hours afterwards, we pitched and rolled and ducked and it poured and it was beastly ... In the middle of the night a big wave made its way into the saloon rousing everybody up ... But one cannot come to sea and always expect calm weather and after a time everything comes to an end.'

On board the *Tutanekai* was Captain Tucker, lessee of Campbell Island, come to check on this most isolated of farms. He was most gratified to find that not only had his flock produced 800 lambs, but that his three men had forty-five bales of wool to load, the hard-earned produce of the past twelve months.

It was now another 400-mile voyage to the Antipodes Islands, to the north-east of Campbell Island: 'A miserable trip to the Island – most people in bed, and not much work for the cook.' As with all other ports of call they had to steam around the islands looking for castaways or wreckage and overhauling the depots. Fortunately the next day dawned bright and calm, a glorious southern morning. The party disembarked, determined to enjoy the weather while they could. Dudley Alexander wrote colourfully to his sister:

> We landed on a penguin rookery, where there was an appalling smell, and
> with difficulty clambered through it up the side of the cliff, surrounded by
> shrieking penguins. At the top ... Albatross were scattered about sitting
> on their nests. They never move and look on quite unconcerned having
> apparently no fear of man.

It was fortunate that they had made the most of the occasion as by the time
the ship reached their next destination, the Bounty Islands, they were in the
middle of a sub-antarctic gale. It was far too rough to consider landing on terrain that was grimly inhospitable even on the best of days. Alexander writes:
'The islands consist of bare rock, covered every inch with penguins and the
smell is appalling.' Undaunted, the government party still carried out their
duties. Lord Ranfurly describes the scene: 'Several times the whistle was blown
with a view of seeing if there was a human being on the rocks. If so we should
have had to stand by till calmer weather with a view to taking them off.' The
official artist was equally dutiful: 'Mr Worsley, no matter what the weather
was, was always at work with his pencil and brush and made a most excellent
sketch when we were "lying to" off the Bounties.' No unfortunate castaways
appeared and they set sail back to Bluff as soon as the gale permitted.

By the time they returned to Bluff on the evening of 26 January, the
viceregal party had covered vast expanses of sub-antarctic ocean. The dis-
tance from Wellington to Bluff was calculated as being 543 miles, while the
journey out and around the southern islands was 2222 miles, most of them
exceedingly rough!

It was now back to work for Lord Ranfurly, while the countess, her daughters Constance and Eileen, Charles Worsley and Captain Alexander ventured
to Mount Cook for several weeks. A time notable not just for the mountains
but for the rain as well: twenty-four inches fell during the time they were there
'which was not considered much'.

A trip up the Tasman Glacier was possibly the highlight of the year.
Certainly these ladies left their mark – two unnamed glaciers were to be
named for them: 'The Lady Ranfurly' and 'The Lady Constance' (now known
as the Ranfurly and the Constance Knox Glaciers). The ten-year-old Lady

Eileen was obviously not yet old enough to attain such icy immortality.

The party started off on horses, temporarily abandoned when they had to cross the Hooker River: the horses forded this while the people were ferried across in a cage (a box suspended on a wire rope – each passenger would then pull himself or herself across). The river safely negotiated, the party made the Ball Hut in six hours. This hut was decently divided into gentlemen's and ladies' quarters. 'The ladies' part just held four bunks and standing room for dressing … proved most comfortable.'

Next morning the party rose at 5.30 a.m. for an early start to a gruelling day. The ladies dressed as practically as convention would allow. Long dresses were certainly *de rigueur*, but some concessions could be made. They all put on their 'coloured goggles and the ladies put on second veils, as the upward glare from the glacier is very trying. We also put large leaves (mountain lily) in and outside our hats as the sun is very fierce.' When stopped for an hour's rest and lunch Constance painted the scene before them, an ice fall where the ice rose very rapidly with crevasses in every direction.

They eventually reached Brodrick's Hut nine and a half hours after leaving Ball Hut. This hut was 5700 feet above sea level and some eleven miles from, and over 2000 feet higher than, the Ball Hut. They dined well as the hut was kept stocked with food and the guides had had the foresight to bring some bread and butter, one bottle of milk and another of whisky. Constance and her daughter 'Puss' were the fourteenth and fifteenth ladies respectively to sleep in Brodrick's Hut.

They had to do more than sleep in it, as the next day dawned with the most atrocious weather: rain, snow, sleet and fog reigned supreme all day. The artists, at least, were well occupied, painting up their sketches or sitting at the open door, warmly wrapped in blankets, trying to make new sketches through the swirling mists. It is not recorded exactly what was eaten, but the menu is likely to have been similar to that presented at the Ball Hut the following evening: 'Liebig Soup, Tinned New Zealand mullet, tinned New Zealand Mutton tongues with New Zealand pickles, sardines on toast, Tinned Colombo pineapple, tea, coffee or whiskey.'

It was fortunate that this expedition was such a success as the weather was bad for the following fortnight of their stay. Constance, however, painted on undeterred, amassing a fine collection of her work before they left. At the end

'Smooth Ice, Tasman Glacier.' Dudley Alexander holds the umbrella to shield Lady Ranfurly as she sketches. Charles Worsley is at the left, sketching the scene. *Dudley Alexander's journal, 1902.*
MSY-4600-038, RANFURLY COLLECTION, ALEXANDER TURNBULL LIBRARY, WELLINGTON.

of their stay a five-horse coach was sent especially from Fairlie to fetch the party. This was, no doubt, more cramped than cosy. 'Three sit on the roof and two next the driver, and room for 6 inside, the luggage on top, under seats etc.'

They rendezvoused with Lord Ranfurly and now made their way further south, staying at sheep stations on their way. The viceregal party admired the countryside, were fed well on turkey (though they would much have preferred to be offered roast merino mutton) and drove through 'barren hills covered with sheep and rabbits'. The rabbits were already frighteningly well-established in these tussock lands. As the party headed through tussock towards Omarama, Dudley Alexander noted: 'From here on, the rabbits are bad for about 200 miles. Several millions are exported from here to England frozen or else tinned. The rabbit skin fetches about 3d. each and is made up at home into all kinds of furs. Felt is also made from the poor Bunny's skin.' On a previous trip to Mataura in Southland the freezing works were full of rabbits – one million were reputed to be waiting for shipment to England.

From here the party headed for the gold-mining towns of Central Otago, ostensibly in casual mode. However, this did not go quite as planned: when they stopped for lunch there were official telegrams to be dealt with and 'though nothing had been mentioned of any functions we were not to be spared'. A school had lined up along the road and been given a special holiday, bouquets were presented to Constance and, once at Cromwell, they were met by the local band, a guard of honour and a welcoming address.

There might have been grumbles in the journals, but the viceregal party accepted everything with typical good grace. Constance held a tea party at their hotel and entertained some forty women: wives of local miners and storekeepers. These humble, hard-working folk were delighted by the countess's attentions. That evening there was a 'conversazione with music'. Dudley Alexander's journal relates:

> We walked around during the intervals of the music talking to our hosts. The Mayoress took C. around and wanted to pass one lady saying she was only the Hotel cook. She however was duly shaken hands with. The Cook was just as good as the Mayoress or the rest of the Company.

The welcome at Alexandra did its best to upstage Cromwell. Two triumphal arches had been raised (one at each end of the main street) and gaily festooned with greenery and flags, the Ranfurly Arms featuring in the centre. Constance dutifully gave another tea party while the Governor was kept busy listening to those who were trying to enlist to fight in South Africa. The seven-foot high postmaster was included in this throng, asking Lord Ranfurly to use his influence to gain an officer's commission as he was much too tall to be a trooper!

Alexandra may have put on a gracious welcome, but it did not agree with Constance. 'Unfortunately C. got seedy at Alexandra. She either was poisoned or suffered from the water there which is not good.' She was miserable all the way to Dunedin where a doctor confined her to bed for some days. Exhaustion may well have contributed to her illness. By the time the countess returned to Wellington (for Easter) she had travelled 3000 miles by sea, 1000 by train and 350 by coach since Christmas.

In 1903 there was great excitement for the family – their nineteen-year-old son and brother Tom, Viscount Northland, joined them in February in an

Lady Ranfurly's farewell at Wellington. 31 October 1903.

official capacity as aide-de-camp to his father. Now a second lieutenant in the Third Battalion of the Coldstream Guards, this was deemed an appropriate point of his career to get some 'colonial experience' and the post an ideal way to combine duty and family. Northland had already spent some time with his family in New Zealand when on holiday from Eton in 1898.

On 14 November 1903 Constance and her two daughters sailed in the *Ionic*, headed for 'Home' after six years in New Zealand. Over this time the countess had entertained many thousands of people of all stations in life and consistently impressed all who met her with her gracious manner, warmth, kindness, lively interest and untiring work for those less privileged.

A farewell ball, held in her honour by the citizens of Auckland, took place in the beautifully decorated drill hall. Some days later two Maori portraits, magnificent oils by Charles Goldie valued at £100 each and purchased by popular subscription, were presented to Constance at an enormous garden party attended by Aucklanders of all classes. 'When the presentation to Lady Ranfurly was made the two pictures were held up in front of the platform, and beside each picture stood the original Maori, whose portrait had been taken.'[1]

There was also an emotional farewell from Wellington. Here a magnificent illuminated 'address' was presented to Constance. When she stood to speak in reply she was so overcome with emotion that Dudley Alexander had to read it in her place. Constance shook the hands of those around her, apologising 'I am so sorry I cannot say anything', tears filling her eyes.

There was no doubt that the countess was greatly admired and loved by the New Zealand people. When she left óne columnist wrote: 'Lady Ranfurly may count herself the most popular of Vice-Queens … Government House, Wellington, has been, under her gentle rule, the centre of many good works as well as of social gaiety.'

Constance Ranfurly left a distinct legacy, not just in the affection and respect in which she was held, but also in all the places, boats and institutions that were named after her. While it was exceptional for other 'lady travellers' to have anything at all named in their honour, in Constance's case there was an embarrassment of riches. She must have had mixed feelings as a glacier, a lodge of female Druids in Wellington, the 'First Battalion Auckland Rifle Volunteers, the Countess of Ranfurly's Own', an oil schooner and a new auxiliary screw schooner built for the fruit trade in the Cook Islands were all named in her honour. Perhaps the most exotic recipient of her name was a famous gold dredge named the *Lady Ranfurly*. In July 1902 this was to set a record of 1234 ounces for a week's dredging. There is no record of the name giving Constance an entitlement to any of the proceeds!

Lord Ranfurly left New Zealand in June 1904 after seven years as the Governor of New Zealand. Also hugely popular, he too left a large legacy in terms of the Ranfurly name. The southern town of Ranfurly is quietly famed, the famous interprovincial rugby trophy, the Ranfurly Shield, hugely popular. An enthusiastic sportsman, Lord Ranfurly would have been delighted to know that this would continue to be keenly contested 100 years later.

On their return to Ireland the Ranfurlys resumed the relative obscurity of the life of the landed Irish aristocracy. They settled back at Northland House where they dedicated one room as the 'New Zealand Room'. The

[1] These paintings, 'The Widow' and 'Darby and Joan', were controversially purchased by the National Art Gallery in 1990 for the sum of $900,000 (over $1 million including GST). They are now held in the collection of the Museum of New Zealand Te Papa Tongarewa, Wellington.

Goldie paintings always held pride of place here, along with the many other mementoes that the Ranfurlys had acquired during their tenure in New Zealand.

Although there are no more scrapbooks full of notes from society pages we can suppose that the Ranfurlys were once again leading lights in Irish society, busy running the estate and involving themselves in the welfare of their tenants. After the end of his term as aide-de-camp to his father, Tom (Viscount Northland) returned to the Coldstream Guards where he was commissioned as a captain. He was killed in action in France in February 1915. His son eventually succeeded to the title.

Both the Ranfurly daughters married military men of impeccable pedigree. In later years 'Puss' (Lady Constance Knox) served as a Woman of the Bedchamber to Queen Mary and as a Lady-in-Waiting to Princess Marina, Duchess of Kent. Lady Eileen Knox was one of Queen Mary's trainbearers at the Coronation in 1911.

Constance, Lady Ranfurly, died, aged seventy-three, on 23 July 1932.

POSTSCRIPT

Dudley Alexander diligently gathered statistics as to how many miles were travelled and how many people entertained during the Ranfurlys' tenure in New Zealand. He worked out that during their time here they entertained 3338 guests to dinner, an average of 557 each year. On top of this they entertained 29,637 guests to 'Balls and miscellaneous entertainments', an average of 4950 each year. The intensity of entertaining was greater some years than others – in 1900 there were no Government House balls as such frivolity was considered inappropriate when New Zealand troops were fighting in South Africa.

BIBLIOGRAPHY

Blackley, Roger. *Goldie*. Auckland: Auckland Art Gallery, David Bateman, 1997.

Burkes Peerage and Baronetage, 106th edition.

Debretts Illustrated Peerage, 1893. In 'British and Irish Biographies', on microfiche.

Alexander Turnbull Library.

Ranfurly Papers. Alexander Turnbull Library.

Scholefield. *Dictionary of New Zealand Biography*. Vol 11, M–Z. Wellington: Department of Internal Affairs, Whitcombe and Tombs, 1940.

MAY KINSEY
1874 – 19??

WHERE SHALL WE GO FOR OUR HOLIDAY? TO THE HERMITAGE, MOUNT COOK? OH NO. IT IS SUCH AN AWFUL PLACE TO REACH AND THE GLACIERS! THEY ARE FRIGHTFULLY DANGEROUS! AND THE PRIVATIONS one has to suffer! Oh no, let us take a quiet three weeks at Sumner. Such are the ideas which prevent people from undertaking one of the most exhilarating holidays to be got on this earth … Both colonists and tourists should have the locality fairly advertised the routes properly described and the comforts and shelters known …

Words written in the 1890s by May Gertrude Kinsey, daughter of exuberant Christchurch businessman, Joseph James Kinsey and his wife Sarah. Certainly more 'Sunday adventurer' than true explorer, May was still a great alpine enthusiast, keen to persuade others to venture into the Alps as she and her family so often did. Once there she revelled in the mountains, climbed some of the smaller peaks, walked at length, enjoyed picnics and shared her Papa's passion for photography.

Mrs May Moore (née Kinsey).
174/1, KINSEY COLLECTION, CANTERBURY MUSEUM, CHRISTCHURCH.

May was probably the most photographed New Zealand 'lady mountaineer' of her time. Ever elegant, May is portrayed chatting to mountaineers of the day, cooking on the camp-fire or climbing a rock face. Other portraits capture her in full climbing regalia outside her alpine bivouac; ice-axe in her hands, a brooch on her satin collar, her hair stylishly topped by her best boater. However, all is not always as it seems: look more closely and you may note the tortured willow, the mowed lawn and the roof in the background. Although some of the bivouac photographs were undoubtedly taken at the Hermitage, others were posed on the front lawn of the family home, destined to impress relatives with tales of holiday adventures. Elsewhere May is depicted in a climbing party that appears to be painstakingly making its way up Tasman Glacier. The picture is highly contrived, all seven in the group stepping out, ice-axes at the ready. However, although the poses may have been staged, the clothes are unlikely to have been donned for special effect. Men and women of standing dressed in much the same manner for drawing room or ice face. Standards had to be maintained.

As the daughter of a very wealthy, energetic, and undoubtedly indulgent father, May was in the privileged position of being able to pursue whatever activities she wished. Always close to her Papa, May leapt at the chance to accompany him on a number of expeditions to Mount Cook during the 1890s. Most of May's social contemporaries are likely to have considered her to be exceptionally intrepid: few women of breeding had either the inclination or the opportunity to venture up glaciers or mountains in the 1890s. May was probably reasonably typical of most women who ventured into the mountains in these early years – keen to 'have a go', but only on the less demanding climbs. In an article for *The Weekly Press* May notes:

> A delightful little climb can be undertaken by ladies to the top of Mount Olivier, 6296 feet. The Hermitage is 2500 feet above sea level, so that this climb is only some 700 feet higher than the top of Mount Herbert, on the other side of Lyttelton Harbour.

Elsewhere May writes, in approving tone, of the new huts built in the alps:

> With such advantages there is no reason why ladies as well as men with a

J. J. Kinsey and climbing party, cutting steps, Tasman Glacier, c. 1890s.
28A, KINSEY COLLECTION, CANTERBURY MUSEUM, CHRISTCHURCH.

Hooker Valley, 1897.
12719, KINSEY COLLECTION,
CANTERBURY MUSEUM,
CHRISTCHURCH.

competent guide should not visit those most distant points on the glaciers which, up to the present, have only been available to the hardy mountaineer ...

May was six years old when the Kinseys immigrated to New Zealand in 1880.
Her father, Joseph, established a shipping agency in Christchurch – a career
quite consistent with his strong nautical background. Business prospered and
Joseph was soon an affluent man, energetically involved in many different
business and cultural circles. The most exotic of his many appointments was
undoubtedly that of Belgian Consul. As a founding member of the
Christchurch Leidertafel, he and other male friends often sang at concerts and
recitals, making friends with many prominent entertainers of the day.

The Kinseys lived a comfortable life that they happily shared with others.
Renowned for their sociability and generous hospitality, they warmly entertained a large variety of visitors in both their city and seaside houses: actors,
actresses, singers, cricketers, admirals and heads of state were among the many
who entered their door. An only child, May would have enjoyed an indulgent

Climbing Party, Mt Cook region. *1914. G. Mannering.*
1498, CANTERBURY MUSEUM,
CHRISTCHURCH.

upbringing, quietly confident in the company of celebrities.

Relatively little is known directly of May – unfortunately no letters or diaries have been preserved to give us an insight into what sort of person she was. However, we do know that she was very close to her father, and shared his love of the outdoors along with his passion for collecting Oriental *objets d'art*, especially beautiful ceramics. Her sense of humour was a worthy match for her father's – May appears as a willing aide in many of her father's humorous photographic endeavours.

Joseph had been introduced to photography by renowned mountaineer and banker George Mannering. A number of albums survive, with some of the most fascinating mountaineering shots dating from 1885–1891 when Mannering and his fellow enthusiasts were climbing many peaks around the Mount Cook area. These photos not only record the peaks and the experienced mountaineers who conquered them, but also show the more amateurish Joseph and May in full climbing clobber.

One visitor to the Kinsey home was a business associate of Joseph's, William Alexander Moore, Australasian manager for Turnbull, Martin and

Co. in Dunedin. This firm acted as agent for the British-based Shire Line of Steamers and it is likely to have been steamer business that initially brought Alexander to the door of Joseph's shipping agency. This dashing, moustachioed Scotsman undoubtedly impressed father and daughter alike. Although we have no clues as to courtship and ne'er a hint of how long it was before romance took precedence over shipping logs, true love undoubtedly triumphed: the *Lyttelton Times* quietly records the marriage of W. Alexander Moore and May Kinsey on 14 June 1900. At the time Alexander was forty years old while May was twenty-six.

Although May moved to Dunedin after her marriage, she continued to make regular trips home to visit her parents. Joseph acted as attorney for both Captain Robert Scott and Sir Ernest Shackleton during their Antarctic expeditions as well as helping to look after the officers and arranging picnics for the crew. He also allowed the expedition photographers to use his darkroom – vast numbers of Antarctic prints and copies of negatives by Ponting, Hurley, Evans and Wilson feature in the Kinsey photographic collection. Even if May was not present on occasions when Antarctic expeditionaries were entertained in lavish Kinsey style, she is sure to have been regaled with tales of their extraordinary adventures.

The Scotts certainly received some exceptional treatment at 'The Den', the Kinsey cliff-top home near Sumner beach outside Christchurch. A special stone platform was built on the cliff edge to allow Mrs (later Lady) Scott to safely watch the bird life below. Scott himself was afforded rather less luxury – as part of his preparations for the trip south, he slept outside in the stone garden shelter. Almost one hundred years on, the garden still retains an Antarctic legacy. The garden paths and plots are bordered by lava from Mount Erebus, brought back as ballast on the *Terra Nova*.

Joseph wasn't just hospitable – he also contributed significant sums of money to the Antarctic journeys. His generous support for the polar expeditions was officially recognised, firstly when he was awarded the Scott Medal by the Royal Geographical Society in 1914, and more grandly when he was created a Knight Bachelor in 1917.

Although May appears to have travelled little after her marriage, as a

Mrs May J. Moore, daughter of J. J. Kinsey.

J. J. Kinsey and his daughter May Moore (née Kinsey) riding Kinsey's 'bicycle built for two', *c*. 1900.
10492, KINSEY COLLECTION, CANTERBURY MUSEUM, CHRISTCHURCH.

member of the Kinsey family she is likely to have met other great adventurers of the age. In the 1930s Jean Batten, Admiral Byrd and George Bernard Shaw and his family were all entertained by Sir Joseph and Lady Kinsey.

On her annual visits to Christchurch, May would bring her little daughter Victoria to spend time with her doting grandparents. For years they would always sign the visitors' book, signatures often accompanied by a new photograph of Victoria. Then, in 1910, a sad little entry records her death. There were no other children.

We know little else about May except that in 1940 she and her mother presented Sir Joseph's collections of books, art, Oriental ceramics and photographs to the nation. May's mother, Lady Kinsey, died the following year. The death of May's only child meant that there were no family members to enjoy the legacy of Sir Joseph James Kinsey and his adventurous daughter.

BIBLIOGRAPHY

Gordon. 'A Russian dog-handler whose home was Clifton.' *The Press*, 22 November, 1975.

Kinsey, J. J. and Kinsey, M. 'Mount Cook and its Glaciers.' Christchurch: *The Weekly Press and New Zealand Referee*, 1897.

Woodward, Joan. 'Sir Joseph Kinsey, 1852–1936.' Notes prepared to accompany an exhibition at Canterbury Museum (unpublished and undated).

FREDA DU FAUR
1882 – 1935

FROM THE MOMENT MY EYES RESTED ON THE SNOW-CLAD ALPS I WORSHIPPED THEIR BEAUTY AND WAS FILLED WITH A PASSIONATE LONG- ING TO TOUCH THOSE SHINING SNOWS, TO CLIMB TO THEIR HEIGHTS OF silence and solitude, and feel myself one with the mighty forces around me. The great peaks towering into the sky before me touched a chord that all the wonders of my own land had never set vibrating.

So wrote Freda Du Faur when describing the first time she gazed at the mountains around Mount Cook. As far as she was concerned the die was now cast – the mountains were all that truly mattered. Once her passion for the snowy peaks was awakened it became a pivotal point of her life, and moun- taineering something she was compelled to do.

She further wrote:

... the true mountaineer, like the poet, is born, not made ... the over-mas- tering love of the mountains is something which wells up from within and

Freda Du Faur. *G Mannering, 1895.*

will not be denied. An unsympathetic environment and want of opportunity may keep this love hidden even from its possessor; but alter the environment and give the opportunity and the climber will climb as naturally as the sparks fly upward.

Emmeline Freda Du Faur was Australian born, the daughter of noted patron of exploration and arts, the wealthy Sydney stock, station and land agent Frederick Eccleston Du Faur. Her mother, Blanche, was the daughter of Professor Woolley, liberal theologian and one-time Professor of Classics at the new University of Sydney. In keeping with this strong tradition of achievement the Du Faurs ensured that Freda received an excellent education, and she attended the Sydney Church of England Girls' Grammar School. Here Freda studied a wide range of subjects including English, geography, history, the classics, French, music, art and drawing. Although Freda enjoyed sports, read extensively and revelled in playing popular tunes on the piano, she was rather less enthusiastic when it came to knitting socks and making samplers to encourage Australian soldiers in the Boer War. No exams were sat – these were considered too burdensome for young minds!

Even at a youthful age Freda's spare time was caught up with challenging physical activities. From the time she turned seventeen the Du Faurs lived in Edwardian comfort in the suburb of Turramurra close to what is now the Ku-ring-gai Chase National Park, a twenty-five-square-mile Government reserve north of Sydney. Freda loved this area and, lured by the flowers, she roamed extensively among the sandstone valleys and bush-clad ridges with just her little dog 'Possie' for company. During the next five years she explored at length, developing her rock-climbing skills as she went.

Freda's father, Frederick, was a fellow of the Royal Geographical Society of London, and the first chairman of the Geographical Society of Australia. Ever interested in Antarctica, he wrote a paper on 'The effect of Polar Ice on the weather' and was later involved with raising money for Mawson's Antarctic expedition. In addition to these interests he was a strong advocate for the establishment of the Ku-ring-gai Chase reserve, and was appointed managing trustee when it was dedicated as a national park in 1894. With this background it is hardly surprising that Freda was always drawn to adventure in the great outdoors.

However, a career was seen as desirable and, at the age of twenty-one, Freda began training as a nurse. Although she undertook this 'for love of the profession', the reality of nursing wore her out. After just two months Freda found herself in sole charge of a seriously ill patient for sixteen hours or more. She was also responsible for cleaning up vomit, emptying toilet pans and washing bodies, both dead and alive. With the combination of such gruelling work and lack of time to read, socialise or even think, Freda became increasingly exhausted. After just a few months she asked to be released from her duties on the grounds of ill health. 'I came out of hospital a wreck, simply because the mental strain on a sensitive, highly strung nature had been too great.' Fortunately her parents were sufficiently well-to-do to make a serious career unnecessary.

Freda spent a number of summer holidays with cousins on their farm near Otaki in the North Island of New Zealand. However, as a far glimpse of the white cone of Mount Egmont was the closest she got to indulging in alpine pursuits, these early trips did little to fuel her love of the mountains. All changed when, in 1906, Freda ventured south for the Christchurch Exhibition. Here she came across photographs and paintings of snowy mountains and met a number of people who had spent time in the Southern Alps. The temptation was irresistible – she deserted the exhibition and headed south for the snow.

Once at the Hermitage, the hotel and mountaineering base for the Mount Cook area, Freda immediately approached the chief guide, Peter Graham, to ask what a novice could attempt. To her joy, he asked her to join a party he was taking up the Sealy Range the following day. This party included Charles Worsley, the painter who had accompanied Lord and Lady Ranfurly's party on their second trip to the sub-antarctic islands and later to the Hermitage.

When the party first reached the snow Freda was exuberantly excited, throwing herself into it, digging it out with her hands and then throwing it into the air with abandoned delight. Then, once she saw the summit, she raced ahead of the others to get there first. She was not disappointed: 'Soon I stood alone on the crest of the range, and felt for the first time that wonderful thrill of happiness and triumph which repays the mountaineer in one moment for hours of toil and hardship.' Peter Graham recollects: 'It was Miss Du Faur's introduction to mountains and her first contact with snow. She was so thrilled with the glissade down the snow slope that she climbed up to do it again.' Life was never going to be the same.

Unfortunately an urgent telegram was waiting for her back at the Hermitage: Freda was called away because her mother was very ill. There were to be no more climbs this season. However, she left promising to return in two years. Sadly, Freda's mother died before Freda returned to Sydney.

The fortnight Freda spent in the area when she returned during the summer of 1908–1909 served as an excellent apprenticeship for more challenging climbs. After one strenuous day Peter Graham commented favourably on her fitness: 'I found Miss Du Faur to be very active; she appeared to have thoroughly enjoyed the walk and was certainly less affected by the tramp up the glacier than the rest of the party ... she was anxious to test herself to see if she had any real ability for serious climbing.' When Peter took her out to practise on the rocks behind the hut he was further impressed by Freda's ability. All those years of scrambling on sandstone cliffs in the Ku-ring-gai Chase stood her in excellent stead.

The following week Freda joined a party that climbed over the Ball Pass. This provided a moment of true inspiration. Freda stood on the summit of the pass, gazing up towards Mount Cook and suddenly knew exactly what she wanted to do. 'There and then I decided I would be a real mountaineer, and some day be the first woman to climb Mount Cook.'

Freda returned to the Hermitage at the beginning of the 1909–1910 season, keen to engage Peter Graham's services before he was caught up with the rush of Christmas visitors. Travelling here was no mean feat. For a start, Freda was a poor sailor: 'I am ever unhappy at sea, so the less said of the five days' voyage the better. The fact that I willingly undergo such days of misery every year may give some idea of how deep is my devotion to New Zealand.'

From the port of Lyttelton Freda continued her journey by train, the rattle of the wheels echoing 'a joyous refrain, "Mountain bound, mountain bound!"' She reached Fairlie in the gathering darkness, delighted to take her 'first keen breath of mountain air'. The next morning she set off on the final stage of the journey, 'a motor drive of 90 miles. Perched on the box-seat and tingling with joyous excitement, I left behind me all the worries of everyday life and felt free and irresponsible as the wind that stung my cheek.'

Eventually she arrived at her longed-for destination ...

Top: Cars bound for the Hermitage outside the Gladstone Grand Hotel, Fairlie.
F-2387-1/2, ALEXANDER TURNBULL LIBRARY, WELLINGTON.

Bottom: The Hermitage, Mount Cook.
29A, J.J. KINSEY COLLECTION, CANTERBURY MUSEUM, CHRISTCHURCH.

The Hermitage is beautifully situated at an altitude of 2,510 feet near the terminal face of the Muller Glacier, which winds in a northerly direction under Mount Sefton and the other peaks of the dividing range. The front of the hotel affords a beautiful view of Mount Sefton, and a few minutes' walk from the back brings one to a fine view-point for Mount Cook.

This was Freda's first serious mountaineering season and she took to it with admirable determination and success. Her début as a serious climber was not, however, without controversy. The initial problem was her planned ascent of Mount Sealy, an expedition that was to involve a night away alone with her guide, Peter Graham. Freda, her mind entirely set on her climbing, saw nothing wrong with this and happily explained her plans to other guests at the Hermitage. The other women went into agitated huddles, seriously concerned as to how such behaviour would compromise the reputation of 'a girl, travelling alone' and forthrightly expressed their concerns to Freda. She was unimpressed.

I found myself up against all the cherished conventions of the middle-aged. In vain I argued and pointed out that I had come to the mountains to climb, not to sit on the veranda and admire the view. If I were to limit my climbs to occasions on which I could induce another woman or man to accompany me, I might as well take the next boat home. At the moment there was no one in the hotel who could or would climb Mount Sealy; there was not the ghost of a climber on the premises, only women who found a two-mile walk quite sufficient for their powers. This they could not deny, but they assured me in all seriousness that if I went out alone with a guide I would lose my reputation.

The fact that the guide in question was Peter Graham, whose reputation as a man was one at which the most rigid moralist could not cavil, made no difference. They acknowledged it was true, but seemed absolutely incapable of applying it to the facts of the case. One old lady implored me with tears in her eyes not to 'spoil my life for so small a thing as climbing a mountain'!

Extremely annoyed, Freda replied forthrightly, 'If my reputation were so fragile a thing that it would not bear such a test, then I would be very well rid of a useless article.' Freda hardly knew what to do, for once even lamenting her single state:

> ... for about ten minutes I almost succeeded in wishing that I possessed that useful appendage to a woman climber, a husband. However, I concluded sadly that he would probably consider climbing unfeminine, and so my last state might be worse than my first.

Despite such apparent bravado, Freda was sensitive enough to realise that her reputation did matter and, as a compromise, reluctantly agreed to hire a porter as well as a guide so that respectability could be preserved. This would cost an extra pound a day. 'I agreed to this, but felt vindictive when I thought of the extra expense entailed, and threatened to send the bill to my tormentors.' It was very frustrating:

> I sighed, not for the first time in my existence, over the limits imposed upon me by the mere fact that I was unfortunate enough to be born a woman. I would like to see a man asked to pay for something he neither needed nor wanted, when he had been hoarding up every penny so that he need not be cramped for want of funds.

She later added:

> I don't wish to pose as a martyr, but merely to point out the disadvantages of being a woman pioneer even in the colonies, where we are supposed to be so much less conventional than elsewhere. I was the first unmarried woman who had wanted to climb in New Zealand, and in consequence I received all the hard knocks until one day when I awoke more or less famous in the mountaineering world, after which I could and did do exactly as seemed to me best.

Peter Graham recollected that Freda 'was very angry at the time. Fortunately she had a rare sense of humour and later saw the funny side of it.' However, he was hardly surprised at the reaction of the other guests. As he later writes: 'In those early years at the Hermitage it was rather rare to meet a woman travelling without a companion of any kind, and if one did so she was invariably looked upon by the other guests as being eccentric – perhaps more so than was in fact the case.' If mere travellers could cause eyebrows to be raised, those women who insisted on not just climbing, but doing so unchaperoned, were definitely defying convention.

The women at the Hermitage may have looked even more askance when Freda returned from her climb of Nun's Veil, triumphant in her exhaustion. Half asleep, she was lifted off her horse at 4.30 in the afternoon and slept till noon the next day. 'When I appeared at lunch the women looked me over and demanded, "Is it worth it?" I was sunburned from brow to chin, and was already beginning to peel. I admitted that it was a pity that mountaineering had such a devastating influence on the complexion, but pointed out that it was only a temporary evil and as nothing to the joys I had acquired at the same time.'

Her next climbs of the season were of Mount Malte Brun and then two peaks known as the Minarets. This last she found to be so challenging that she mentally thanked her brothers for years of 'training':

> Backwards and forwards we dodged amongst great blocks and pinnacles of ice which sagged and leaned at drunken angles as if they meant to fall and bury us for evermore. To me the whole place was an icy nightmare, recalling to memory horrid pictures ... in Dante's 'Inferno', where poor tormented souls shivered in awful depths of internal ice ... My mind was chaos, my nerves on edge, but fortunately neither of these are exposed to an unsympathetic world; and my face, thanks to the long training of two brothers who jeered at me for a girl baby if I dared funk anything, was no doubt smiling and bland.

When, later that season, Peter decided that Freda was fit enough to attempt Mount Cook, the second guide had to pull out at the last moment due to a poisoned arm. After much discussion Peter decided that Freda was by now a strong enough climber to be able to make the climb alone with him. A porter was in the party so the moral doyennes of the Hermitage were quietened. However, this time it was the self-appointed 'guardians of safe climbing' who were very unhappy. These good men quickly condemned the apparent folly of taking a 'frail' woman on such a climb with just one guide. Even the highly respected pioneering mountaineer, Jack Clarke, entered the fray. Freda wrote indignantly: 'If he would simply ignore the fact that I was a woman, and judge me as an individual on my climbing merits, the case might appear to him in a less alarming light.' She and Peter remained firm in their resolve and made their attempt, unfortunately foiled when they found a huge schrund (a gap between a rock and snow ridge and the top of a glacier) cutting off access to the route they had chosen. Given the controversy surrounding the climb this was an unfortunate blow to Freda's feminist soul, 'one of the bitterest moments I ever experienced'. She was going to have to wait another season to achieve her dream.

Clothing was another point of contention. Although some earlier climbers such as Constance Barnicoat had climbed in full boy's garb, this mode of dress became harder to adopt in subsequent years. As the Hermitage became an increasingly popular tourist destination there were more people to see and disapprove of what mountaineering women wore – few dared risk the disapprobation of the social establishment. Although the daring climbed in calf length skirts many mountaineering ladies still favoured long skirts, often down to their heels, in combination with elegant blouses, jackets and hats. Sturdy boots were generally worn and long veils used to protect their faces from the sun.

When fitting out women wearing these long skirts Peter Graham gave them a piece of cord to tie around their waists so they could pull the skirt through it to a convenient length – this was all secured by safety pins. Peter carried a supply of these pins and was insistent that, for issues of safety, skirts must be shortened by some inches. If this seemed a little risqué to some, the necessary adaptation for glissading was positively indecent.

'For glissading, women's skirts were drawn back through the legs and tucked firmly in front fastened with a safety pin.' One terribly proper lady climber, the mysterious 'Lady B' submitted meekly to the procedure and then:

> … sat down in the groove made by the others and we were off. In the forward movement her skirt was pushed up to show more leg than she approved of, and in her efforts to remedy matters her heels caught in the snow and she wheeled round hard with her legs now pointing skywards …

She was furious and asked that we stop at once as it was quite disgusting.

Freda was certainly not going to let herself be hobbled by such impractical attire. She compromised by wearing knickerbockers, conveniently covered by a knee length skirt wryly described by Peter Graham as a 'frill'. However, she still dressed in a distinctly feminine manner. The photos of Freda standing with an ice-axe and posing with her guides, Peter and Alex Graham, show a turnout that seems too elegant for the mountain. However, she was genuinely in climbing gear, though minus her coat. A photo of Freda on top of Mount Dampier shows her in knickerbockers, short skirt, white high-collared blouse and buttoned woollen jacket, all topped by a hat and veil.

Freda also 'improved' her mountain attire from time to time, with the cheerful addition of the New Zealand edelweiss, 'their fat little white flowers and silver-grey leaves peeped out of every nook and cranny with a cheerful optimism that was infectious. We gathered a handful and decorated our hat-bands.'

It was not just impractical clothing that added to the challenge of alpine climbing. Although some foreign alpinists had set the trend of putting nails on the soles of their boots, crampons were not yet worn in New Zealand. This made climbing icy slopes extremely challenging – the guides had to cut steps in the ice, a labour-intensive and exhausting job that made many ascents extremely slow. The Graham brothers were step cutters par excellence who skilfully wielded extremely heavy, long-handled adzed ice-axes for hours at a time.

In preparation for the ascent of Mount Cook, Freda and her two guides, Peter and Alex Graham, climbed up to the Hooker Hut to wait for the right weather. The morning of 2 December 1910 dawned fine and calm. Freda writes:

> … we set off at 5.15 a.m. Both the Grahams were heavily laden with about 50-lb swags. In vain I remonstrated; they were determined I should have every luxury as well as necessity, and they would not lighten them by so much as a pound. No woman ever had two more kind, considerate, and trusty companions.

'On the Summit of Dampier. Miss Du Faur & her guide, C Milne, who with Peter Graham who took the photo, are the first to reach this spot. Above is seen the great final snow slope of Cook.' Weekly Press, 1 May 1912.
13108, WEEKLY PRESS PHOTOGRAPH, CANTERBURY MUSEUM, CHRISTCHURCH.

The route initially led up the Hooker Glacier and icefall to their campsite on the upper Hooker. Here they began to fix the bivouac and prepare for the next momentous day, 3 December 1910.

> The guides set off to kick steps for the morning, so that we could start before dawn; returning about 5.30 p.m., they reported everything in a most satisfactory state. They had walked over the schrund at the junction of rock and snow which had blocked us the year before, and followed up a snow couloir for about 1,000 feet. These steps would save us some stiff rock-work in the morning and about an hour in point of time. Cheered by such news as this, dinner was a jubilant meal; and after it was over we crawled into our sleeping bags as a protection against the evening chill and waited for sunset.

On earlier climbs Freda had been disadvantaged as 'decency' dictated that she slept in a separate tent from the guides, a much colder option than sharing accommodation. By the time she made her second attempt to climb Mount Cook she had decided that this was impracticable. She is unlikely to have discussed her new sleeping arrangements with the ladies of the Hermitage:

> The evening turned exceedingly cold, and I decided that having already walked over most of the conventions since I began mountaineering, one more would matter nothing; so I suggested to the guides that they abandon their tent and save me from shivering in icy aloofness till morning.

> The plan worked well, and I really got some sleep, especially in the early morning when Alex lit the two "cookers" inside the tent, and a delicious sense of warmth and luxury, pervaded by a smell of methylated spirit, stole over me. The next I knew was a polite request to wake up and eat breakfast at 1 a.m.

They set off at 2.45 a.m.:

Freda Du Faur with guides Alex and Peter Graham. *G. Mannering.*
14352, CANTERBURY MUSEUM, CHRISTCHURCH.

It was bright starlight, perfectly calm, and very cold. We put on the rope, lit two lanterns, and started away, Peter leading, I in the middle, and Alex bringing up the rear. The lanterns cast just enough light to show the previous night's steps. The snow was frozen very hard, and in the dim light seemed to slope away to fathomless depths.

Once they were within a few feet of the top Freda was sent on ahead.

I gained the summit and waited for them, feeling very little, very lonely, and much inclined to cry. They caught my hands and shook them, their eyes glowing with pleasure and pride, and with an effort I swallowed the lump in my throat and laughed instead. Then we all began talking at once; it was only 8.40 a.m., and we had beaten any previous record by two hours, and I a mere woman! I felt bewildered, and could not realize that the goal I had dreamed of and striven for for years was beneath my feet. I turned to them with a flash and asked if it were 'really, truly the summit of Mount Cook,' whereat they laughed very much and bade me look. Truly we were on top of the world, our little island world. Nothing impeded the eye – east, west, north and south the country unrolled itself at our feet …

The weather was superb and the views glorious – Freda was allowed to enjoy this to the maximum extent. The billy was boiled and the three climbers celebrated their ascent with a high-altitude picnic and a two-hour rest.

The way down was not quite so straightforward. A piece of 'rotten' rock hit Freda, bruising her back and then, a little further down, a large block of rock gave way under her feet. She was held safely by the guide above, but was shaken nevertheless. When they stopped to rest Freda noted 'the Grahams looking furtively at me, and [I] knew as well as if they had spoken that they were wondering how much more I could stand. As I did not know myself, I pretended not to see their glances, and drank down some hot tea and ate a little with thankfulness.'

She need not have worried. The rest of the descent was made without significant incident. Once safely down they whooped with joy and raced towards their bivouac, 'laughing and excited like so many schoolchildren'. Suddenly Freda was stopped:

Peter caught my hand and Alex stood beside me smiling, 'Now we will congratulate you, now we are safe down and have beaten all previous records, Look!' and drawing out his watch he pointed to the time, 5.30 p.m. 'By Jove! six hours up, two hours there, six and half down; that time will take some beating, little lady,' and Alex shook my other hand vigorously. 'Thanks to the two finest guides in the mountains, it will,' I answered.

Back at the Hermitage the next afternoon Freda found herself an instant celebrity.

Telegrams and cables came pouring in ... from members of the Government and an Admiral of the Fleet to unknown and unheard-of admirers in out-of-the-way towns came congratulations in every shape and form. In fact for the first time of my existence I was famous. Needless to say I enjoyed it; as for Peter and Alex, with every fresh wire ... their smiles grew broader. Vainly they tried to keep a countenance of everyday solemnity, but a word dissolved them into the proud trainers of a prize pupil.

Freda enjoyed debunking myths, and never more so than on this triumphant night:

Being perfectly well aware that the average person's idea of a woman capable of real mountaineering or any sport demanding physical fitness and good staying power, is a masculine-looking female with short hair, a loud voice and large feet, it always gives me particular pleasure to upset this preconceived picture. In the year of grace 1910 a love of fresh air and exercise is not a purely masculine prerogative ... and should be quite easily associated with a love of beauty and personal daintiness ...

She goes on to write of the pleasure of returning to civilization and 'clothes which combine beauty with utility. Consequently, I strolled out to dinner immaculate in my prettiest frock, and so supported was able to face the hotel full of curious strangers and the toasts and congratulations that were the order of the evening.'

Freda was certainly not going to rest on her laurels – they were in the middle of the climbing season and she didn't intend to waste any time relaxing. It was only a matter of a few days before she and Alex Graham set off once more, this time to climb Mount De la Beche, 'a sharp snow-and-rock cone immediately south of the Minarets on the western side of the Tasman Glacier'.

This expedition really just served to fill in time until Peter Graham could join them in another momentous climb. Mount Cook behind her, Freda now wanted to be the first woman to climb Mount Tasman, generally regarded as the most difficult ice-climb in the Southern Alps. They were somewhat delayed by bad weather, but by the evening of 15 December, just eleven days after their triumphant return from the ascent of Mount Cook, Freda, Peter and Alex were bivouacked under a large boulder near the top of Haast ridge. The next morning they set out at 1.30 a.m. As the sun rose they could look straight up the Linda route on Mount Cook. 'This looked in such excellent condition that we were almost tempted to abandon Mount Tasman and see if it was not possible to complete the Rev. W. S. Green's route to the summit of Mount Cook.'

Tempted or not, they decided to continue with their initial plan to climb Mount Tasman. They may have later regretted this perseverance as, unlike the previous ascents of the season, this was to prove a disappointing climb. The ridge they had to navigate looked gentle enough from below, but on closer inspection Freda reported 'it rears a knifelike edge for 1,000 feet at the most appalling angle I had ever beheld or imagined ... Here and there on the ... ridge shone unmistakable patches of ice, leaving us no illusions as to the kind of ascent we were up against.'

This ridge had only been climbed on one previous occasion – in reasonably good snow conditions. This time it was solid ice, meaning that steps had to be cut all the way. Progress was painfully slow and conditions deteriorating. Pragmatism eventually had to triumph over ambition and the party turned back.

It was a most nerve-racking proceeding. The ridge was so hard that it was impossible to dig the point of the ice-axe into it; it was simply a question of lowering one's self down from one slippery step to another with nothing but the moral support of the rope to rely upon ... The wind blew clouds of drift snow about us, and often it was necessary for each of us in

J.B.'s First Glissade. *William Spotswood Green, 1879.*
E-581-Q-054, ALEXANDER TURNBULL LIBRARY, WELLINGTON.

turn to stoop down and clear the snow from the half-filled ice steps before we dare set foot on them. The wet rope, rigid and stiff like iron, was also difficult to manage. On one particularly bad portion my nerve deserted me somewhat, and I found I could not manage the descent with my face to the abyss below me. After several tentative attempts I turned my face to the arête and let myself down backwards, practically straddling the ridge from step to step. Above me Peter waited with the rope taut, a worried line between his eyes. Below me stood Alex, his face a mixture of horror and amusement at such an unorthodox proceeding.

It says a lot for the relationship between Freda and her guides that they took her on such climbs at all, respecting and trusting her mountaineering skill and instincts. She writes in appreciation:

The Grahams were splendid in the faith they always showed in my moun-taineering powers. After the season's teaching, trying and testing, they always took my ability for granted, no matter what difficulties we encountered. Perhaps one of them would give me a quiet suggestion if they thought it would be useful, but I was never worried or teased with minute directions. Their unvarying confidence in me has been one of the great elements in my many successes. It has often spurred me on to bigger efforts, where a want of confidence would simply have crumpled me up and made me lose faith in myself.

On another occasion Freda writes of the training she received from Peter Graham.

> Graham has a theory on the best way to train a novice into full-fledged mountaineer ... he considers that it gives the minimum of risk and the maximum of pleasure to be led from climb to climb, each of increasing difficulty, until one is fit physically and mentally for the most difficult and dangerous work. He did not deny ... that he might be able to take me up Mount Cook at once, but he did deny that I would get the highest benefit and pleasure out of the experience. 'Climb Mount Cook at once,' he argued, 'and you will have done what is considered the biggest climb in New Zealand, therefore you will have nothing left to look forward to here ... Except the mere notoriety of being the first woman on the summit, you will gain nothing, and stand to lose the best of a wonderful experience, because you have tried to grasp it before you are ready to appreciate it in all its fullness.

Freda not only climbed, she also included skiing in her repertoire. On 29 December 1910 she joined a party skiing on the Darwin Glacier. 'All of us were novices, consequently we went where and how the skis chose, not where we desired. This led to much hilarity ...'

Just two days later Freda's friend, Muriel Cadogan, arrived for a holiday. A strong, clear-eyed woman with thick brown hair, Muriel was a physical training instructor, one of two 'Lady Experts' employed at the Dupain Institute of Physical Education in Sydney. Prior to her return to the Hermitage for this climbing season, Freda had spent three months training at the Institute under Muriel's care. 'I emerged from my quarter of strenuous work, under Miss Cadogan's capable hand; fit for anything, and with a reserve fund of endurance to call on …'

As the friendship between the two women developed, Freda had become increasingly interested in Muriel's 'feminine theories' and also came to rely heavily on her commonsense and abundant energy. Freda adored Muriel from an early stage, relishing her company above all other, even naming a peak 'Mount Cadogan' in her honour. This is the only close relationship that Freda is known to have had. Shared tents or not, there was never a hint of any romance with any man – to Freda they were good climbing mates and trusted friends, but never anything more. Those moral doyennes at the Hermitage need not have concerned themselves.

Although the two women later lived for many years as a committed lesbian couple, at this point the relationship had yet to develop physically. Sally Irwin, Freda's biographer, notes: 'Freda was then still just another breathless heroine with a "best chum".' Two memorable weeks followed. Freda and Muriel ventured forth in the wettest of weather, togged themselves up in oil-skins and picnicked under rocks – soaking or not, this seemed much better than being cooped up in the crowded Hermitage. Once the weather dawned fine, Freda dragged Muriel out in the early hours so she could gain her first glimpse of the glorious mountains. 'Her sympathetic understanding was all I expected it to be, and I felt infinitely the richer by a thoroughly sympathetic companion, the first in all my seasons in the mountains.'

Over the next couple of weeks Freda introduced Muriel to the joys of mountaineering, initiating her into the delights of climbing and glissading alike. 'I lived my first mountaineering hours over again as I watched my friend gallantly struggling to gain her equilibrium as she shot down the steep slope.' There were picnics and ice-axe training followed by a joint expedition to the Ball Hut before Freda went off to climb yet another mountain. A stunningly beautiful bivouac by Sealy Tarn was marred by the attentions of keas (mountain parrots) whose pestering impudence drove the women back into their tent. Even worse, they pulled Freda's precious Kodak camera into the lake, a great dampener to the spirits.

Muriel enjoyed the mountains so much that by the time they left Freda was delighted to report: 'I saw every sign of her catching the mountaineering fever badly and was thereat greatly rejoiced.'

Freda may have climbed the highest mountain in New Zealand, but

she still felt worthy challenges lay in front of her. Her attempt to return the following January (1912) was almost thwarted when her father met with a serious accident. 'For some time I was unable to procure the services of a trained nurse, and by the time I eventually did so and my father was convalescent I was on the edge of a nervous breakdown.' Luckily their understanding doctor immediately sent her off on holiday so Freda returned to the Hermitage in February, eager for yet more peaks to climb. The first, a 7860 foot peak near the Copland Pass, Peter Graham named Du Faur in her honour. This was a great compliment from the leading guide of the day.

This was quickly followed by a first ascent of another yet-unnamed peak. Freda called this Nazomi 'which according to Freda, is Japanese for "heart's desire"'.

The next mountain of moment was Mount Tasman – Freda and the Grahams were determined not to be beaten on this, their second attempt. The climb was a gruelling affair:

> ... so cold that in five minutes one of my gloves was frozen to a solid ball of ice at the finger-tips and I lost all feeling on the left, or west, side of my nose ... I called out, 'Go on; I can stand it if we can get shelter soon.' So we went in the teeth of the wind and across the ridge. The snow slope was steep, so they cut out a hole for me to sit in and another wherein to rest my feet, and then took places on either side of me and helped to thaw out my frozen fingers ... We were soon beautifully warm, and began to consider what we were to do next.

They crossed the schrund on the way to the top by standing on each others' shoulders and pulling themselves up with ice-axes. This was one of the toughest of all Freda's climbs – in freezing wind it took them five hours to climb just 600 feet.

The following season, the summer of 1912–1913, presented one of the greatest challenges in New Zealand climbing. Freda set out with Peter Graham and another guide, Darby Thomson, to make the 'Grand Traverse', the first traverse of all three peaks of Mount Cook.

First attempt 'Nazomie'.

13107, WEEKLY PRESS PHOTOGRAPH, CANTERBURY MUSEUM, CHRISTCHURCH.

The climb went very well, an epic twenty hours from beginning to end. Peter Graham later notes: 'Mountaineers today regard this feat as one of the finest in the history of the Southern Alps. No crampons were worn, and the step cutting in ice demanded extraordinary endurance.' Unfortunately, however, the party suffered from sunburn and a shortage of water. Peter Graham describes:

> Our thirst increased, and we gave way to this and ate ice. This made us thirstier, and it was rather unfortunate for Miss Du Faur because her lips swelled badly afterwards ... In the morning, Miss Du Faur's lips had swollen so much she was in some distress; how would she look on arriving at The Hermitage? On my insistence she bathed them before leaving camp, and again at the Ball Hut.

Although the swelling had gone down a little before their return it was still a problem. Freda records:

> We arrived at the Hermitage at 4.30 p.m. and were greeted with cheers from the assembled household. I still had a handkerchief over the lower portion of my face, which apparently caused some consternation. One imaginative tourist set the theory going that I had all my teeth knocked out by a falling stone. I managed to mumble a decided denial to this theory, and escaped to try what hot water foments would do for me. By dinnertime I was not normal but quite presentable, and was glad to appear in public and enjoy the congratulations on our successful ascent.

> The whole thing had been done so quickly and simply that sometimes I found myself wondering how it had all come about. Providence certainly does seem to favour my Cook climbs – to walk out of the Hermitage without any fuss and conquer the greatest climb in New Zealand at the first attempt, and return in the best of health and spirits two days afterwards, was undoubtedly rather an extraordinary feat. My guides were so proud and pleased, the Hermitage would hardly hold them, and they had the pleasure of saying, 'I told you so' (which is not a purely female prerogative) to their doubting and now envious brethren, who had professed that nothing but disaster would come of such a risky expedition.

Freda's enthusiasm was matched by the pragmatic skill and experience of her guides and she writes:

> I would like to record my gratitude and appreciation of my guides, Peter Graham and David Thomson, who staked their lives and reputations on the expedition. Theirs is the real triumph; they planned and thought out and led the expedition to a triumphant finish; their knowledge and hard won experience, their courage and endurance made it possible.

Despite this extraordinary feat and Freda's other impressive climbing achievements, there were some who felt that, as a woman, she should not be taking on some of the more difficult climbs. When the traverse of Mount Sefton was being discussed, Peter was approached by an old friend with a kind word. 'You know, Peter, if I were you I don't think I'd like to take a woman up Sefton.' Peter was undeterred and 'duly arranged with Miss Du Faur who was always a "goer" – you only had to suggest a thing and she would be with you – to set out and have a look at the mountain'. The 'look' encouraged them and they reached the summit a few days later, subsequently descending it in dreadful conditions.

Food on these expeditions must have been a challenge; but the provisioning and cooking were always ably looked after by Freda's guides. Thermos flasks of tea are a recurring theme, along with wine biscuits, chocolate, cheese, figs, oranges and tins of peaches and pineapple. Empty whitebait tins, with names and date inscribed, are stashed in stone cairns. On their descent from Mount Cook the Grahams prepared a veritable feast of savoury tomato soup, cold meat, tinned fruit and bread and butter, the cooking done on methylated spirits cookers, and everything washed down with freshly brewed tea. Tins of 'Brand's essence' were carried in case of emergency. On the one occasion Freda resorted to this mysterious brew she found it so nasty that she left the rest for her guide.

Although we are given few descriptions of the food, the context of it was a different matter. Triumphant after their ascent of Mount Sealy, Freda recalls:

> Supper was a meal to remember; seated on a rucksac, with my back to a rock, I enjoyed every moment of it. The red flames lit up the brown faces and gleaming eyes and teeth of the guides as they plied me with one good

thing after another, and the whole made a picture worthy of Rembrandt.

The one time Freda does mention her own cooking, general competence is implied for all but dessert. 'The process was conducive to much laughter; with the exception of a blancmange of tempting appearance but unfortunate solidity, the result was up to the somewhat ambitious standard set by the previous chef.'

As tourism grew and the road to the Hermitage became steadily busier, the old cob and iron building was no longer adequate. However, not all were happy when the new building was begun. Seasoned visitors mourned the loss of the old Hermitage. Freda prophesied sadly that 'the big new hotel' would be a 'fashionable place with tennis courts, golf links, etc., where you will have to dress for dinner and play about in pretty clothes – in fact, a fashionable tourist resort'. She much preferred the 'old, happy, carefree, home-like days spent in the ugly rambling cottage building'.

They may have disapproved, but there was no arguing with nature. It is unlikely that anything could have withstood what came down on the Hermitage at the end of Freda's last New Zealand climbing season in early 1913. Torrential rain breached the Mueller moraine and the flooded Mueller River swept down towards the building, bearing rocks, ice and trees along with torrents of water. Freda later described seeing 'a yellow flood coming straight for us, sweeping everything before it'.

Initially the threat of the Hermitage being actually flooded seemed minimal: although the hotel was surrounded by water, the force of the torrent was bypassing it. The guests dined as usual and went to bed – a mere flood may have seemed a minor problem for hardy men and women of the mountains. Then the flood changed direction. Freda recounts:

In the dim hours of the early morning I was awakened by a terrific crash; it sounded as if Mount Sefton was falling into the valley, and shook the house from end to end. I tumbled out of bed, slipped on a coat, and flew down the hall. The lamps were all alight and the drawing-room filled with a shivering, whitefaced crowd and their most cherished possessions. The water was flowing under the front door and over the floor of the new building [the wooden additions to the original cob structure, known as the annexe] ... fitful flashings of lightning and the first gleams of daylight

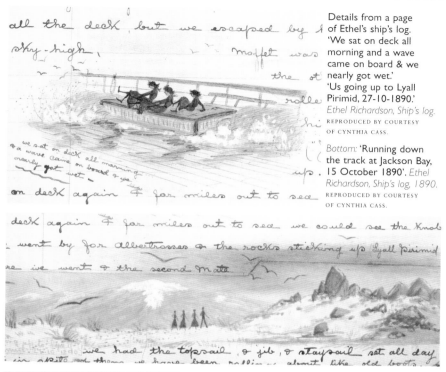

all the deck, but we escaped by ... sky-high, ... moffet was ... the ot ... rolle ...

we sat on deck all morning & a wave came on board & we nearly got wet –

on deck again & far miles out to sea

Details from a page of Ethel's ship's log. 'We sat on deck all morning and a wave came on board & we nearly got wet.' 'Us going up to Lyall Pirimid, 27-10-1890.' *Ethel Richardson, Ship's log.* REPRODUCED BY COURTESY OF CYNTHIA CASS.

Bottom: 'Running down the track at Jackson Bay, 15 October 1890'. *Ethel Richardson, Ship's log, 1890.* REPRODUCED BY COURTESY OF CYNTHIA CASS.

deck again & far miles out to sea we could see the Knob
went by for allbertrosses & the rocks sticking up Lyall Pirimid
re we went & the second Mate
we had the topsail, & jib, & staysail set all day
... them we have been rolling about like old boots.

Running down the track at Jacksons Bay,

Top: **Campbell Island.** *Countess of Ranfurly, 1902.*

Bottom: **Macquarie Island – Wreck of the** *Gratitude. Charles Worsley, 1902.*

The viceregal party climbing through penguin colony.

Mount Cook. *William Mathew Hodgkins, 1875.*
Publ-0016-32-CT, MUSEUM OF NEW ZEALAND TE PAPA TONGAREWA, WELLINGTON.

showed a raging torrent sweeping beneath the annexe and gurgling through the piers on which the building is raised. The roar that had waked me was the grinding together of a great mass of boulders swept down from the Mueller moraine … and deposited not ten yards from the front door.

The building survived this, but not for long. A few weeks later, in March 1913, twenty-four inches of rain fell in twenty hours. The Mueller River roared down its new flood channel, full force onto the hotel, undermining and breaking off the annexe and damaging the main building beyond practical repair. Not even the most enthusiastic lovers of the old Hermitage could now campaign for its retention.

There were other changes too, ones that Freda certainly considered to be for the better. Now some four years after her first tussles with self-appointed protectors of her reputation, she was a famous mountaineer, greatly admired and certainly respectable. At last she could 'do exactly as seemed to me best'. Even better, she notes that 'the girl climber at the Hermitage need expect nothing worse than raised eyebrows when she starts out unchaperoned and clad in climbing costume'. This was a triumph indeed.

During this last season at the Hermitage Freda was already planning to go to live in England. There were probably two quite different reasons why she did not plan yet another summer in the Southern Alps. The first was that she had done it all: Freda had climbed the hardest climbs, set records, and named mountains. She writes: 'Life was "flat, stale, and unprofitable". All the dreams and plans that had filled my days with speculations and excitement were over, the "glory and the dream" had passed into prosaic reality.'

Freda had loved the challenge, but the most difficult was done. It was time to move on to other challenging alpine areas. She certainly knew that she was not returning. After completing the 'Grand Traverse' she wrote: 'From the other side of the world I shall eagerly watch and wait in the years to come to see who will be the next party to thread their way over that long icy ridge.'

The second, and probably more compelling, reason was that she wanted to go to England with Muriel. Better career prospects for Muriel, new climbing challenges, the appeal of the Suffragist movement and the prospect of independence from family demands, all combined to make this a desirable move for the two women. Now thirty-three years old, Freda moved to England in 1914.

In England Muriel became involved with the London Society of the Suffragettes while Freda worked on her book, *The Conquest of Mount Cook and Other Climbs*, a fascinating account of her New Zealand climbing career, dedicated lovingly to Muriel. By the time this was published Freda was describing their relationship as one of 'hedonistic inversion', the popular term for lesbianism. The women moved to Red Cottage, a charming house in Pinner on the outskirts of London, and settled down to as much domestic harmony as the First World War would allow. Freda worked as a volunteer nurse, took up painting and, with Muriel, provided a welcome haven for family and friends.

One New Zealand friend, fellow climber Erica Westmacott, later reported that Freda and Muriel lived in a 'very close relationship, like a married couple'. She was rather more shocked to find that Freda, ever her heroine, was quietly keeping house, mountaineering little more than a far memory. The war in Europe had inevitably put paid to many mountaineers' ambitions, but there were more complicated issues involved for Freda. Although Freda optimistically wrote: 'Some day, if my dreams come true, I hope to tackle some of the giants of the Himalayas', she never climbed again after leaving New Zealand. Once in England she was entirely deterred by the fact that women were not allowed to join the English Alpine Club. Although there was the Ladies' Alpine Club, this was not good enough – Freda wanted acceptance by what she saw as the only true club. She would not compromise her principles even if it meant no climbing.

The rest of Freda's life makes dismal reading. She and Muriel went back to Australia briefly in 1919 but returned to England by the following year. Opportunities seemed better in Britain, and it was easier for women to live as a couple in the old world society. Times were hard but Freda's private means cushioned them from some of the harsh realities of post war depression and they bought a house in Bournemouth on the south coast. Painting filled much of Freda's time, while Muriel pursued her interests in fitness and parapsychology.

However, Muriel was increasingly mentally unstable, and in 1928 was admitted (or perhaps committed) to a rest home where Freda also stayed. Both Muriel and Freda appear to have been drugged and given 'deep sleep therapy' (a 'rest cure') and Muriel may have been given electro-shock therapy. Such treatment was popular to alleviate symptoms of mental disturbance and may also have been an attempt to 'cure' the women's lesbian tendencies. Freda was forbidden to see the increasingly ill Muriel who was dispatched back to family in Sydney in June of 1928. Unfortunately she never made it – Muriel died, supposedly of 'Heat Prostration', as the ship passed through the Bay of Biscay.

The collapse of the stockmarket in 1929 meant that Freda's finances were as fragile as her mental health, giving her even more to worry about. Plagued by imaginary voices and increasingly paranoid, she returned to Australia for the last time in 1933. Here she lived at Dee Why, north of Sydney, at first with her brother and his family and then in her own cottage. Her main interests appear to have been the same as those which sustained her from an early age – enjoying the outdoors, bushwalking in the nearby area and socialising with her small circle of friends and family.

Unfortunately this was not enough to lift Freda from her obvious depression – family remember her at this time as being noticeably withdrawn and lonely. In the end her existence must have seemed to lose its point – she no longer had a great love or momentous challenge to live for. On the night of 10 September 1935 Freda wrote a letter of explanation and placed it with a box of her most treasured belongings. She then turned on the gas and put her head in the oven, dying in the early hours of September 11. She was just a few days short of her 53rd birthday.

BIBLIOGRAPHY

Australian Dictionary of Biography. Vol 4, 1851–1890, and Vol 8, 1891–1939. Melbourne: Melbourne University Press, 1972 and 1981.

Du Faur, Freda. The Conquest of Mount Cook and Other Climbs. London: Allen and Unwin, 1915; Christchurch: Allen and Unwin, 1977.

Graham, Alec and Wilson, Jim. Uncle Alec and the Grahams of Franz Josef. Dunedin: John McIndoe, 1983.

Graham, Peter. Peter Graham: Mountain Guide, an Autobiography. Wellington, Auckland, Sydney: A. H. & A.W. Reed, 1965.

Irwin, Sally. Between Heaven and Earth. The Life of a Mountaineer, Freda Du Faur. Victoria: White Crane Press, 2000.

Lynch, Pip. 'Scaling the Heights, They Called it "An Easy Day for a Lady".' NZ Women's Studies Journal, Vol 3, No 1, August 1986.

Macdonald, Charlotte, Penfold, Merimeri and Williams, Bridget. The Book of New Zealand Women. Wellington: Bridget Williams Books, 1991.

Ross, Malcolm. A Climber in New Zealand. London: Edward Arnold, 1914.

NZ Herald, 9 June 1984.

Wilson, Jim. Aorangi, the Story of Mount Cook. Christchurch: Whitcombe and Tombs Ltd, 1968.

CONSTANCE BARNICOAT
1872 – 1922

'WAR CORRESPONDENT, TRAVELLER, ALPINIST AND IMPERIALIST'

… SKIRTS, EVEN THE SHORTEST, ARE ALMOST IMPRACTICABLE IN SUCH PLACES … I PROMPTLY SENT FOR PROPER BOY'S BOOTS, THE HEAVIEST PROCURABLE, WITH VERY THICK SOLES WHICH I HAD WELL NAILED, AND generally rigged myself out as much like a boy as possible with a white wool 'sweater', knickers, and puttees to my knees. Except in some such dress the guide flatly refused the risk of taking ladies; and he was perfectly justified.

I wonder if anyone realizes, until they try it, the freedom of being without tempestuous petticoats? Whatever arguments may be urged against a boy's dress for a woman anywhere within range of civilization, those arguments do not hold good in wilds such as we went through … A real boy's dress is, in my view, far preferable in every way to a compromise such as a so-called 'reformed' costume . . .

So wrote Constance Barnicoat as she enthusiastically regaled readers of *Wide World Magazine* with details of how she crossed the Copland Pass. Such func-

Constance when she crossed the Copland Pass. 1903.
CONSTANCE GRANDE, BY JULIAN GRANDE, CHAPMAN AND HALL, LONDON, 1925.

197

tional dress for women was radical stuff back in 1903, some seven years before the legendary Freda Du Faur had her well-publicised tussles with convention over climbing attire. No such nonsense for the formidable Constance Barnicoat – this lady alpinist was practicality itself, entirely intolerant of inhibiting social proprieties.

And she was not without role models. In Europe there was the stylish example of Mlle Henriette d'Angeville, forty-four years old when in 1838 she became the first woman to climb Mont Blanc. This intrepid lady adapted her attire with stunning style: red flannel underwear, Scottish tweed knickerbockers lined with flannel, a fur-lined hat and a star bonnet, a veil, green-tinted spectacles, and a plaid, carrying 'the indispensable alpenstock' all the while. Mlle Henriette appears to have bowed to convention more as the years passed – when she made her last climb some twenty-five years later (aged sixty-nine) she wore a crinoline!

Similarly, early Taranaki settler Jane Maria Atkinson had no hesitation in flouting convention for her historic climb of Mount Egmont in 1855. Far too sensible a lady to consider long skirts for a mountain climb, Maria had a pair of 'dungaree or canvas trousers' made expressly for the occasion. Such practical daring was entirely out of line with the conventional clothing favoured by other adventuring women of the day. Another mountaineer, Bessie Ross, wore trousers on Mt Earnslaw in 1892 and on the Milford Track in 1895 but wore a calf-length skirt for later climbs from the Hermitage.

Certainly by 1895 most women climbing in the Southern Alps of New Zealand were making some concessions, practicality slowly edging its way into feminine climbing attire. Those in the forefront of daring fashion stepped out in skirts raised to three or four inches above the ankle – these were worn in elegant combination with small boots, jackets, blouses and wide-brimmed hats. This shortened skirt, while hardly sensible climber's attire, greatly increased safety and general manoeuvrability.

Such an outfit was still not considered appropriate by the emancipated Constance, though this in part appears to be due to the hard line taken on climbing dress by her no-nonsense guide. The inclusion of two knickerbockered women in the party may also have made this 'boy's attire' more easily acceptable – there was both safety and respectability in numbers.

Constance Barnicoat was born in Nelson in 1872, the seventh child of

Constance Barnicoat, aged three. November 1875.
12599/2, NELSON PROVINCIAL MUSEUM, NELSON.

'Ashfield', the Barnicoats' home near Richmond in Nelson. c. 1930–1950.
LHB 26, NELSON PROVINCIAL MUSEUM, NELSON.

Cornish immigrant John Wallis Barnicoat and his wife Rebecca. A surveyor, John Barnicoat had arrived in Nelson in 1842, one of the earliest settlers to come to the fledgling settlement.

The following year John was involved in a hotly disputed land survey at Wairau in what became the province of Marlborough. Resistance from local Maori had been strong, prompting John and others to come from Nelson to enforce possession of the land. When the local police magistrate tried to arrest the chiefs Te Rauparaha and Te Rangihaeata on 17 June 1843, shots were soon exchanged. Then, in what became known as the 'Wairau Incident', twenty-two Pakeha and four Maori were killed. John Barnicoat was lucky to escape unscathed.

The following year John was also involved in the selection of the site for Dunedin – fortunately a less dramatic chapter in this surveyor's tale. Meantime he settled on land at Richmond, just out of Nelson, and established the Barnicoat property of Ashfield. From here he continued to work ceaselessly for the good of the province, always strongly involved in the Provincial Council of Nelson, the Anglican Church and the Education Board.

John's wife Rebecca had come to New Zealand as a twelve-year-old, enduring some exceptionally grim days in the early Nelson settlement with her family – they had to rely on gifts of money, agricultural implements and clothes from English relatives just to keep them going. Constance writes: 'At one time, so hopeless and emaciated did my grandfather and the elder boys become with their exhausting labours and insufficient food, that they almost began to lose heart.' When, little more than a year later, Rebecca's father died 'of a broken heart' there was neither money to bury him nor any food in the house. Rebecca was just eighteen at this point – her fiancé, the thirty-five-year-old John Barnicoat, supplied money to buy the coffin.

When Julian Grande wrote of Constance's family many years later he noted that:

> Their spirit of adventure became like oxygen in her blood, and while her own early life was comparatively sheltered and free from care, the imagination of all the dangers encountered and almost incredible hardships endured by her nearest and dearest ones of an older generation did much to mould her own quiet, persevering, indomitable nature, giving her mind a bent and relish for equally real, if somewhat diverse, wanderings, hardships and perils.

A warm, clever woman, Rebecca and her husband were remembered with huge affection by a childhood friend of her daughter, one of the Fell sisters.

> Mrs Barnicoat so motherly with her round figure and hair parted in the middle ... and Mr Barnicoat as courtly and polite as a chevalier out of a dream. We were actually asked what we thought of this and that, and as Constance held forth nineteen to the dozen we found our tongues too. I always had a marvellous sense of well-being there – well fed, treated like a human being, kissed and made much of.

Constance was brought up in this exceptionally loving home, receiving the best of attention and encouragement in everything she did. Riding was a particular passion: Constance was an enthusiastic horsewoman from a young age,

Right: **Constance, aged 16.**
CONSTANCE GRANDE, BY JULIAN GRANDE,
CHAPMAN AND HALL, LONDON, 1925.

Below: **Nelson College for Girls – girls
playing tennis in front of the school.**
Tyree Photo, 1889.
T8X10 1269 181886/3, NELSON PROVINCIAL
MUSEUM, NELSON.

renowned as much for her daring as for her undoubted skill.

Not only was the Barnicoat household renowned for its warm and happy atmosphere, it also boasted a pretty garden, expansive green fields, plantations of trees and a beach on the border of the property. The Fell girls remembered that some of their happiest Saturdays were spent here. 'The garden at Ashfield was full of roses, and at the back there were fowls, and a dear old long-haired dog, and ducks in the pond … [a] cheerful homey place.' The girls would jump over tidal channels, roll on the grass with laughter and climb walnut trees in typical girlish style. Less typically, the Fells would bring Constance extracts from Virgil to translate for them.

Years later Constance was remembered as a very slight, rather delicate-looking little girl with a long fair pigtail, light blue eyes, a pale complexion and a very clear, incisive way of speaking. She was always dressed very neatly, but she 'was not in the least alarming'. She is further described as 'deeply affectionate, extraordinarily faithful, perfectly self-possessed'.

Constance's siblings later agreed that there was no early indication of their sister's intellectual brilliance. This, to a degree, may have been due to the large age gap between them – Constance was eight years younger than the next youngest, her sister Agnes, and spent much of her time alone. Her emotional self-sufficiency would have been a strength when tragedy marred the young girl's upbringing – Agnes died when Constance was ten and her brother James was killed in a shooting accident some four years later.

Education and learning were always considered to be of paramount importance: every spare evening John Barnicoat would read aloud from the best of the British magazines and reviews: the *Quarterly*, the *Edinburgh*, the *Saturday* and *The Spectator*. In days when more formal educational options were distinctly limited, this was an essential part of the education of the young Barnicoats.

Constance was initially taught at home, learning Latin and French from her father while visiting tutors were responsible for German and more French. Then, when she was fifteen, Nelson Girls' College was opened – Constance spent two years there before going on to excel in English at Canterbury College in Christchurch. She completed her BA degree in 1892. A quite exceptional student, Constance was well remembered by the soon-to-be chancellor of Canterbury College, Professor Macmillan Brown:

Nelson College for Girls Boarders. Constance probably sitting on ground at left of photo.
Tyree Photo, 1889.

I shall not soon forget the first appearance of Miss Constance Barnicoat ... her tall distinguished figure and the vigour of character in her face and movements struck me, and I foresaw that whatever career she chose she would pursue with distinction and success ...

The impression was deepened by her work ... she knew her mind and could express it with lucidity and ease ... she had an inborn taste for greatness of thought and beauty of style ... she found the joy that can be experienced in thinking out a subject on original lines and giving it the most artistic expression ...

As she went out into the world a graduate I had no hesitation in foreseeing that she would take to journalism and in the end map out a fine literary career for herself ... She keenly appreciated the satirical strokes that brought out the germs of degeneracy to be found in modern journalism.

Constance next prepared herself for a literary future by becoming a proficient shorthand writer and typist, essential skills for any journalist. She also spent three years working in the Wellington office of the Crown Solicitor, Francis Dillon Bell. Here Constance gained a comprehensive education in the workings of law and government of both Britain and New Zealand before she set sail for England on May 10 1897 in the steamer *Himalaya*. By now the journey to Europe was relatively speedy – she was in Colombo by 1 June and arrived in London at the end of that month.

Ever thorough, Constance immediately set out to improve her already impressive qualifications – a year at the Metropolitan School for Shorthand and Languages brought her distinction along with fluency in French and German. During this time she was continually required to work in a variety of languages, to write articles for a variety of French magazines and translate innumerable English dispatches for the German-Swiss newspapers.

Although Constance was now exceptionally well prepared for a career in the journalism world, she initially didn't seek work as a journalist proper. Instead she first became 'lady secretary' and then editorial assistant to William T. Stead, editor of the *Review of Reviews*, working for him in one capacity or the other for the next eleven years. This role brought her into the middle of European politics and literature, an extraordinary position for a young lady from colonial Nelson. Constance accompanied Stead to the Hague Peace Conference in 1898 and had an ongoing role in reviewing new books in the major European languages. She also started to work extensively as a journalist in her own right, contributing articles and reviews to many other newspapers including the *Daily Express*, *The Times*, *The Press* (Christchurch), *Empire Review* and the *Ladies' Realm*.

A strong supporter of Stead, Constance was intensely trustworthy and loyal. When approached by an eminent newspaper proprietor keen to discover secret details in the will of Stead's friend, Cecil Rhodes, Constance's response was to the point: 'If I were a man, I would throw you downstairs, but as I am a woman I only ask you to leave the room.' There were no further requests!

The relationship between Constance and Stead was not only a professional one; it also had a strong element of father-daughter affection. She later recalled that when Stead brought Constance news of her father's death in 1905 he was 'very, very kind and tender indeed, and said that he was much more my father now than anyone, which is true'. Then, in 1912 when Constance received the first news of the sinking of the *Titanic*, with Mr Stead among the 2000 passengers on board, she correctly assumed he would not be among the survivors. 'He would do nothing to save himself, he would only think of helping others.'

Living in London must have presented a number of challenges for even the most conventional of young ladies, pragmatically prepared to do things the accepted way. Constance, however, didn't automatically conform. Her independence and energy ever to the fore, she quickly worked out that it was much quicker to commute by bicycle than train or tram. The traffic and weather may have been challenging but, undaunted, Constance biked from her rooms in Battersea to Fleet St every day.

Travelling of every sort was of interest to the intrepid Constance. Hot-air balloons were at the cutting edge of aviation technology, a topical source of amazement: Constance lost no time in arranging a flight, along with one Rev. Bacon 'well equipped with bombs for sound experiments'. They flew right across London, gained directions by shouting to onlookers below, tangled in telegraph wires and went up to the giddy heights of 3000 feet before delighting assorted royal children by landing in Windsor Park. 'We seemed to be sailing on a sea of clouds … a very rough sea it was, with great billows of white clouds, just like the waves of a stormy sea, only that they were almost still, and all pearly white or tinged with faint purple … one did not seem to be in the world at all.'

When Constance's mother became very ill towards the end of 1902 Constance took leave from her job and set sail home to Nelson, sadly arriving after her mother's death. Most of 1903 was spent back in New Zealand, dutifully with family and friends and, more adventurously, exploring the mountains. This was to be the introduction to a new passion – mountaineering.

On 3 April 1903 Constance, a Miss Ada Perkins and the indomitable Mrs Jane Thomson,[1] both of Greymouth, became the first women to cross from the Hermitage to Westland via the Copland Pass. The famed Mount Cook guide,

[1] Jane Thomson was the second New Zealand-born woman to climb Mount Cook – she reached the summit in 1916 at the age of fifty-seven. Legend tells that when her guide dallied with attractive young ladies in the Hooker Hut, Jane went in after him, dragged him out by his ear, pushed a pack at him and told him to get started. He meekly did as he was told! Years later, at the age of seventy-one, she was the first woman to climb Mount Rolleston.

First women to cross Copland Pass, 1903. L–R standing: Constance Barnicoat, J. Smith (guide), J. Clarke (guide), Jane Thomson, W. Tennent (?). Kneeling in front: Ada Perkins.
WAK203 12321, W.A. KENNEDY COLLECTION, CANTERBURY MUSEUM, CHRISTCHURCH.

Peter Graham, tells of passing their party.

> Mrs Thomson asked me if we had seen a lady passing ahead of them. We replied that we had seen someone but we did not know whether it was a man or a woman. Mrs Thomson laughed at this and said it was understandable as Miss Barnicoat was wearing men's clothes. Guide Clarke had fitted her out in one of his climbing suits before she left the Hermitage … It had rather startled the inhabitants along the Coast to see a woman travelling in such attire.

As an article written later by Constance relates, this trip was hardly a gentle introduction for a novice climber.

Single file through the snow.

Of course before attempting such an expedition as ours, of the extreme roughness of which it is very difficult, almost impossible to give an idea to anyone unacquainted with trackless virgin country, I had to satisfy the guide that I was fit for the undertaking. At first he shook his head. 'Very well,' I thought, 'you shall shake your head another way before I have done with you,' which he did. I spent over a fortnight at the Hermitage training as hard as I could about the mountains and moraines and up the great eighteen-mile-long Tasman glacier.

On the second day of the crossing this training was well tested.

> ... about eleven the snow of the Copland Pass was reached. For nearly an hour we were roped together, three and four, the guide cutting steps in the ice and trying the snow with the axe to test its safety. The scene was the bleakest and most desolate conceivable – nothing but snow, mist, and bare rocks all around, the snow often knee deep, the wind icy and cold, and

everything soaking and wringing wet. Yet, in spite of wet and cold, it was an absolutely fascinating experience that I have longed ever since to repeat. No mishaps occurred; no one rolled down the ice slope; and about mid-day the Copland Pass (seven thousand one hundred and eighty feet) had been for the first time crossed by women, in honour of which we shook hands all round with our guides, and everyone drank everyone else's health, all amongst the snow and ice, in the thick drizzle and biting wind.

Although it is not recorded what they drank their health in, we do know that Constance routinely carried brandy on later European climbs. That versatile hipflask of 'medicinal' brandy could have a multitude of applications!

From Andrew Scott's accommodation house on the West Coast Constance made her way to Hokitika.

I managed it in five days by pushing ahead at full speed, mostly by riding, generally on a man's saddle this being the only way of getting about that part of the country because of the perpetual un-bridged rivers. Some of the way I rode a high-geared man's bicycle that by great good fortune I hired from one of the scattered settlers' houses. Only one woman had bicycled over the same ground before and I do not think many will do so again. It is beyond everything tough, and, somehow or other, your bicycle has to be got over the bridgeless rivers or, worse still, the rickety suspension bridges ... Generally in these regions you must be prepared for two things – to rough it as in all probability you never did before, and to receive more unfailing and universal kindness than in all certainty you ever did before or ever will again.

Constance was hooked and climbing now became a grand passion. Once returned to her life in London it was inevitable that she would turn her eyes to the European Alps for future adventures.

Constance's first European climbing holiday in 1905 involved the ascent of three major French peaks. Typically, she avoided anything that could be seen as easy or 'suitable for ladies' – her approach was quite the opposite. She later wrote that the first peak, the Ailefroide, 'attracted me particularly because no woman had ever ascended or crossed it, from either side, because

Constance on the Great Schreckhorn in 1911. With Julian Grande and guide. This is the picture that appeared in the London papers the day after Constance and Julian's wedding.
CONSTANCE GRANDE, BY JULIAN GRANDE, CHAPMAN AND HALL, LONDON, 1925.

it has so far been very rarely done ... and because it is reputed extremely tiring. I had afterwards cause to know that its reputation in this respect was richly deserved.' After her successful climb of the Ailefroide, Constance looked immediately to the Meije, inevitably appealing as it 'has had its very fair share of victims, and is reputed to be the worst all round peak in Europe, whose ascent and crossing is a kind of hall mark of alpinism'.

Constance prepared well for her expeditions. She not only dressed practically, she also had her alpine menu down to a fine art.

I am not one of those people who cannot eat on mountain tops, and I generally take just what my guides have – Gruyère cheese, a little cold meat, sometimes tinned tongue, bread and jelly, biscuits, and tinned pears, the last too costly a luxury to be allowed except on summits. As extras I always have quantities of sugar and prunes, peppermint lozenges, and peppermint essence. I carry brandy, but rarely use it.

The following year Constance climbed in the Pyrenees, 'worth seeing once' but no true rival to the Alps. A 1907 trip to the Caucasus saw her travelling for days in Russian trains, sleeping in a Tartar village in an area 'more or less dangerous and lawless' and lying ill in her tent for three days, stoically enduring extremes of scorching sun and freezing glacier winds 'far worse than I have had to endure elsewhere'. Although Constance recovered sufficiently to explore at least some of the Caucasian valleys, climbing mountains was out of the question in her weakened state. She sent her two guides to climb the 18,000 foot high Mount Elbruz but was disappointed not to be able to do it herself as 'everyone has their mountain-sickness height ... and I wanted to find out whether 18,000 feet and over had any incapacitating effect on me'.

On this trip Constance was accompanied by two Italian guides, brothers from a well-known Matterhorn guiding family. Not only were there no other 'ladies' in the party, there were no 'gentlemen' either to protect Constance's reputation. However, the question of impropriety is never raised – obviously Constance was so formidable that her honour was never an issue!

The following year she climbed in the Asturias in northern Spain, three days and two nights by train from London. This expedition particularly appealed because she was 'the first English woman really to penetrate into the heart of the Asturian mountains'. Here Constance also had the unexpected pleasure of chamois hunting with the Spanish aristocracy.

In January 1911 Constance made her most challenging climb to date, a winter ascent of the Great Schreckhorn in Switzerland. This was not as lonely an affair as previous expeditions had been – this time Constance was advised by a Mr Julian Grande who not only engaged her guides for the sixteen-hour climb, but also accompanied her for part of the way. Constance and Julian had met the previous year when Constance reported on Julian's own mid-winter ascent of the Great Schreckhorn to her various papers. Handsome, very charming, intellectually brilliant and a competent linguist, Julian was also a journalist, contributing extensively to a variety of leading English-language papers.

Details of their courtship are not revealed, but there is little doubt that the couple were mutually smitten. Julian married the thirty-nine-year-old Constance in London on 28 March 1911, only a matter of weeks after Constance's triumphant winter ascent. Although the wedding was small, the marriage of two such distinguished mountaineering journalists was an

Mr and Mrs Julian Grande.
CONSTANCE GRANDE, BY JULIAN GRANDE, CHAPMAN AND HALL, LONDON, 1925.

irresistible story for the media. Some two hours after the ceremony the first editions of the evening papers already featured the wedding. The accounts in the morning papers added their portrait and a photograph of them roped together on the Great Schreckhorn.

It is probable that only a fellow mountaineer, and an exceptionally intelligent one at that, could have sufficiently impressed Constance for her to consider even a relationship, let alone marriage. This love of the mountains, their journalistic careers and their mutual commitment to the British Empire drew the couple together into what Julian later described as 'that kind of marriage which is made in heaven'. Julian adored Constance: *Constance Grande: War Correspondent, Traveller, Alpinist and Imperialist*, the biography he wrote after his wife died just ten years after their marriage, is written in adulatory style. He understood and admired both her formidable intellect and indomitable spirit and also relished the way in which they often worked together on projects. Ever generous in his praise, Julian's male ego never appeared to be in the least bit threatened by the continual achievements of his quite remarkable wife.

There is no doubt that Constance was a forthright person, entirely intolerant of fools and frauds. Julian writes: 'Absolute sincerity was the ruling note of Mrs Grande's character. She never could bear pretentiousness of any kind. "I can forgive anything but hypocrisy," she would often say. "They bore me," was her verdict on people who gave themselves any airs.'

Constance's suitability as a feminist role model is in some question as she saw herself as an individual apart. Not only did she not set out to pave the way for other women to follow in her footsteps, but at times she expressed strong reservations as to their fundamental suitability to do so. Although Constance loved mountaineering, she did not generally regard it as a suitable occupation for women:

I am prepared for contradiction, and even abuse from feminists, when I state that the number of women who have climbed throughout a long series of years, long enough for them to acquire any real skill or knowledge of mountains and glaciers, always has been and still is exceedingly small ... few women have a sufficiently sound physical constitution or sufficient physical strength ever to become first-rate climbers. Absolute soundness is probably more essential to the mountaineer than great physical strength ... and how many women are absolutely sound, physically strong and really enduring?

... but given a good guide and a sufficiently strong, healthy woman, who should be thin, muscular and in good training even before starting on her holiday, I think nothing so invigorating, refreshing and fortifying as mountaineering, nothing so helpful in building one up to face another hard year's work in dismal London ...

... among women climbers there are a few Greathearts ... who may hold up their heads with most men climbers ... After this chosen few, there are many Ready-to-Halts, who go on for a few years ... but not long enough to attain real skill or knowledge of the mountains.

Mountaineering expeditions aside, Constance was an impassioned traveller, always restless to visit exotic lands. Over the years she travelled to Bavaria,

Egypt (she and Julian dined with Lord Kitchener), Lapland (thirty-nine and a half hours by train), and the Argentine, (including a twenty-two-mile ride in deluging rain and tropical heat to see the Yguasu Falls from the Brazilian side).

Wherever she travelled and lived Constance never ceased to be a great lover of New Zealand and her southern heritage. However, although Constance often wrote positively of the land of her origin, she could be equally critical. New Zealand children especially concerned Constance, childless herself and used to the well-disciplined Swiss of her adopted land.

> There is one feature which every visitor to the colony notices without fail ... I refer, of course, to the rampageous character of most of the children. One wonders if they really are the worst brought up in the world. Parental control is very slight, and the disrespectful way in which parents seem to allow their children to treat them must have caused many an English visitor ... to make big eyes. The usual excuse – that the children are so much with their parents – will not hold water ... when children have been allowed to run riot and behave as they like for the first six or eight years of their lives, the mischief is done, and no one need ever think that any amount of care and trouble in the future will entirely undo it ...

> Educationally New Zealand has a reputation which ... on the whole, is higher than it deserves ... Secondary education suffers from too much democracy ... this tends to lower the standard of teachers selected, too many of whom are socially and in every way inferior to many of their pupils, at whose houses they would never visit.

Her concern that 'one of the chief drawbacks of a colonial upbringing is that it often tends to a lack of interest in the outside world' led to her instituting the Barnicoat Essay Prize for the boys' and girls' colleges in Nelson. This competition was calculated to encourage the study of contemporary world history.

And then there was her concern for the unnerving change that was happening to the English language in these outposts of Empire: 'Everyone ... is prepared for the colonial twang – an evil worse in some parts of New Zealand than in others, but increasing everywhere ...' Such frank views about aspects of New Zealand life earned the comment that Constance 'was a competent journalist and rather terrible'.

When the Grandes returned from Palestine in the summer of 1912 they lived briefly in London before settling in Switzerland. The prospect of war was beginning to loom over Europe and, in typical style, Constance was drawn to where the action was most likely to be. After some discussion she told Julian: 'Switzerland will be either the battleground or the plotting-ground of Europe; let us go there and we shall be at the centre of things.'

The prospect was irresistible and in the spring of 1913 the Grandes moved to Berne, capital of Switzerland, to 'our home ... on the ground floor of what would be in England called a semi-detached villa, with a garden in front and at one side, and a little strip behind as well. It is almost in the country, for all around are large houses standing in fair-sized gardens, gay with flowers ...'

Once there the Grandes settled into a gruelling work schedule. During the war years Constance worked voluntarily an average of sixteen hours a day on behalf of British propaganda. Julian later wrote:

> My wife maintained a relentless literary fire upon the ... enemies of the cause of Britain and the Allies ... She always fought with clean weapons, and never condescended to write the word "Hun" or "Boche". Convinced of the absolute justice of the Entente cause, she contended for it with all her might. I know not how many thousands of dispatches she sent to the dozen papers ... with which we were connected. Her working day was never less ... than sixteen hours, Sundays and other days being nearly alike. And when the war had been won, she worked as hard for [an]other four years to win the peace. Then her work was done.

Constance's perfect command of French and German and her competency in Spanish and Italian gave her the opportunity to enjoy and critique a wide variety of European literature. That apart, her work was not what one might expect of a 'lady journalist' in these pre-emancipation years. Although she did write of their life in Switzerland, Constance would never have deigned to write 'suitable' articles on knitting patterns, servant management, gardens or gossip. For both her and Julian, work meant anti-propaganda articles such as 'In the Plotting Ground of Europe – How German Propaganda was counteracted', dispatches designed to prevent the English Labour Party from opposing compulsory service and a whole series of anti-propaganda books and pamphlets. These were many and varied, including a glossy book on *German Prisoners of War in Great Britain*, 'The British Fleet in War Time', 'Ypres, the City of the Dead', and 'The Red Cross and Prisoners' Camps'.

Constance routinely met many of the leading thinkers of the day. She wrote:

> ... having been domiciled in Switzerland since before the war, I have made the personal acquaintance of Lenin, Radek and Trotsky; and during the first years of the war I was frequently in touch with them. My professional duties, indeed, have brought me into contact with all sorts of people in this the plotting ground and also the listening post of Europe ... I used to meet these men sometimes singly, sometimes all three together ... very frequently I used even to take a short walk and have a talk with them ... With Lenin and Radek I believe it would be possible to reason, but not with Trotsky. As for the countless brutal crimes laid to the charge of the former, I cannot think that they are personally guilty of them.

Constance's articles for the Christchurch *Press* were particularly appreciated by her one-time professor, Macmillan Brown.

> Her articles revealed ... how keenly she saw into the heart of European politics. And her insight seemed to go deeper as the war approached and went on. She was evidently in touch with many of the inner sources of diplomacy and political movement ... In Switzerland she seemed to get a bird's-eye view of the great struggle, hearing as she did the reports from all sides through fugitives or escaped captives or the wounded. She was in sympathy with the highest ideals of the Allies, and yet could gauge the thoughts and purposes of the enemies. Some of those articles have clung to my memory by their vividness and prophetic insight. One especially ... describing the vagrant life of Lenin and his fellow revolutionists as she saw it in Berne before they were shot over Germany and the Russian border to do havoc by propaganda in the Russian armies.

> And this phase of her journalistic career culminated in her splendid translation of Nicolai's Biology of War, which must have put heart into

America and England and into the American and English armies, and helped to induce the final effort that drove the enemy back through Belgium ... She was beginning to view the world and history not as a series of unconnected scenes worthy of picturing and recording, but as the evolution of some divine purpose ...

Constance may have been busy writing on issues of Empire and impending war, but she still had time for simple domesticity. Julian's memoir recounts:

Refined simplicity was the characteristic of her home life. In Berne and in Vésenaz she was in this respect, I believe, just what her mother had been in her home in far-off New Zealand. She loved housework, and when her journalistic tasks were finished for the day she turned with pleasure to knitting and sewing. She never smoked even a cigarette.

Elsewhere, Julian writes of how Constance lived her life during their sojourn in Berne:

My wife, although she spent most of her time in reading and writing, always began her day, at latest at 8 a.m., by going through every room in the house with the vacuum cleaner, and brushing the dust from the cornices, arranging with the maid about the meals of the day, and putting fresh flowers in the vases of the different rooms. Each of her two maids, who were brought up in Bernese farm-houses, was not only taught by her to lay a table in English style and polish silver, but instructed in English cooking, from the preparing of a roast beef to the various kinds of English puddings ...

As regards sewing and mending, too, my wife liked to do everything with her own hands. Throughout our married life she never spent more than £40 or £50 a year on dresses.

Constance had two 'tasteful and dignified' dresses made each year by a Genevese dressmaker, but would only order what Julian approved of. Ever the devoted husband, he always accompanied Constance to the dressmaker or milliner:

Leptospermum scoparium. Manuka. Constance's favourite flower. *Georgina Burne Hetley.*
B-073-015, ALEXANDER TURNBULL LIBRARY, WELLINGTON.

... and even on the choosing of a veil I had to give my verdict. On the other hand I made her choose the material and shade of all my clothes and the colour and shape of my felt hats. In a word, she never neglected any of the womanly graces. While she was not a 'Hausfrau' she was certainly the very antipodes of what used to be called a bluestocking.

Always a lover of flowers, Constance was especially charmed by the delights of the alpine regions. 'I have gathered rhododendrons in the Caucasus and great blue iris in the Pyrenees, snow-white ranunculus with golden centres in the New Zealand Alps, and fragile pansies, pale sky-blue Alpine forget-me-nots, and pink rhododendrons in the European Alps ... The loveliest flowers, perhaps, are the highest up – those which grow almost out of the snow itself.' Her favourite New Zealand flower was reputed to be the manuka. Constance loved this so much that she thought it should be New Zealand's national flower.

Towards the end of 1915 Constance's health began to deteriorate. Julian reports, 'One night she was seized with a violent trembling; then her body became rigid and her eyes fixed, so I thought at first she was dead.' Despite the pleas of her specialists Constance refused to take any significant time off work. 'If I perish I perish,' she said and later added to Julian: 'Darling, what does it matter if you and I perish, if only the British Empire be saved.'

She did have to make some concession though: for the next six months Constance lay in bed undergoing treatment from Röntgen-rays[2] for an internal tumour. Rest wasn't an issue – Constance had her typewriter set up on her bed. 'She seemed to think of one thing alone – that the Allies must triumph. Nothing escaped her attention; her active mind was full of dispatches to be sent and articles to be written … her fingers made the machine click as swiftly as ever while she set down the thoughts of her teeming brain.'

The work may have continued, but Constance never recovered sufficiently for more climbing expeditions to be an option. 'Though she gradually regained a measure of strength … in which she lost naught of the zest of life or the enjoyment of Nature, she was never quite the same again, and the unspeakable joy of our climbing days together was over.'

When peace finally came the Grandes spent Armistice Day at home in Berne, without celebrating in the least.

> We could not dance on the graves of millions slain, or sing among living millions stricken in body or broken in heart … I remember how my dear wife sat with head bowed and face covered with her hands as if she were at prayer, while she kept moaning, 'What an end, oh what an end!' She was … unspeakably glad that justice had been done; but sad, infinitely sad that victory left the world in chaos and misery without a parallel.

The war over, the Grandes moved to the new focus of activity – Geneva, centre of the League of Nations. Here they continued to work until the midsummer of 1922, by which time Constance's tumour was causing her so much pain that she could no longer attend sessions of the League. An operation was performed and initially thought to be successful but Constance continued to be feverish and unwell. Visitors to her sick-bed included Sir Francis Dillon Bell, New Zealand Attorney General, who was attending the League

---

[2] Wilhelm Conrad Röntgen 'discovered' X-rays on 8 November 1895. By the turn of the century 'Röntgen-rays' were already well established as a treatment for cancer.

of Nations, and his Grace, the Archbishop of Canterbury, who also spent an hour talking with her.

As the weeks passed it became evident even to Constance that she wasn't getting better.

> She put all her papers in perfect order, and talked with me of my future if I should be left alone. She remained perfectly conscious and observant of everything around her, smiling in her last hour at unuttered thoughts of her own. On September 16 she said to me, 'Lift me up, darling, I find it hard to breathe,' and a moment after I had gently raised her she breathed her last.

Constance was only forty-nine years old, but had achieved and written more than many do in much longer lifetimes. Tributes at her funeral included a wreath of flowers from the head of the German war-time propagandists in Switzerland. In what was perhaps one of the greatest tributes Constance received, this gentleman confessed that during the war he had 'feared Mrs Grande more than all the other British and French propagandists together'. She would have been delighted.

Julian fulfilled one of Constance's dying requests by making a journey to New Zealand, to meet family and friends and see the country of her birth. He especially revelled in the mountains and glaciers of the Southern Alps. When in 1923 Julian climbed a previously unnamed peak among the mountains of Westland, he named it Peak Barnicoat after his beloved wife.

BIBLIOGRAPHY

Barnicoat, C. 'Where No Woman Ever Went Before', *Wide World Magazine*, March 1904, pp. 566-75, Hocken Library.

Grande, Julian. *Constance Grande: War Correspondent, Traveller, Alpinist and Imperialist*. London: Chapman and Hall, 1925.

Lynch, Pip. 'Scaling the Heights. They Called it "An Easy Day for a Lady".' *NZ Women's Studies Journal*, Vol 3, No 1, August 1986.

MacDonald, Charlotte, Penfold, Merimeri and Williams, Bridget. *The Book of New Zealand Women*, Wellington: Bridget Williams Books, 1991.

Porter, Frances. *Born to New Zealand: A Biography of Jane Maria Atkinson*. Wellington: Bridget Williams Books, 1989.

Penguin Books (NZ) Ltd, cnr Airborne and Rosedale Roads,
Albany, Auckland 1310, New Zealand
Penguin Books Ltd, 27 Wrights Lane, London W8 5TZ, England
Penguin Putnam Inc, 375 Hudson Street, New York, NY 10014, United States
Penguin Books Australia Ltd, 487 Maroondah Highway, Ringwood, Australia 3134
Penguin Books Canada Ltd, 10 Alcorn Avenue, Toronto, Ontario,
Canada M4V 3B2
Penguin Books (South Africa) Pty Ltd, 5 Watkins Street, Denver Ext 4,
2094, South Africa
Penguin Books India (P) Ltd, 11, Community Centre, Panchsheel Park,
New Delhi 110 017, India
Penguin Books Ltd, Registered Offices: Harmondsworth, Middlesex, England

First published by Penguin Books (NZ) Ltd, 2001

1 3 5 7 9 10 8 6 4 2

Copyright © Bee Dawson, 2001
Copyright © illustrations, as listed in captions.
Front cover image: Constance when she crossed the Copland Pass. 1903.
Constance Grande, By Julian Grande, Chapman and Hall, London, 1925.
Back cover image: Getty Images.

The right of Bee Dawson to be identified as the author of this work in terms
of section 96 of the Copyright Act 1994 is hereby asserted.

Designed and typeset by Athena Sommerfeld
Printed in Australia by APG, Maryborough

ISBN 0 14 100415 0
www.penguin.co.nz